TAKING WOMEN IN NEW DIRECTIONS

*Stories from the Second Wave
Of the Women's Movement*

From
New Directions for Women
1972–1993

By
Paula Kassell

*To Janet
yours truly for equality.
Paula Kassell
December 2009*

*The Issues
That Galvanized Women
To Change Society
Completely & Forever*

Copyright © 2008 by Paula Kassell

All rights reserved. No part of this publication may be reproduced, stored in or introduced into a retrieval system, or transmitted in any form, or by any means (electronic, mechanical, photocopying, recording, or otherwise), without the prior written permission of both the copyright owner and the publisher of this book. For information address Hudson House Publishing.

Articles reprinted herein originally appeared in *New Directions for Women in New Jersey, New Directions for Women,* and *Morristown* (NJ) *Daily Record.*

Published by Hudson House, Poughkeepsie, New York.

The following illustrations in *New Directions for Women* are reprinted with permission:
Separate and Not Equal in the Workplace by National Association for Female Executives, Spring 1979.
Cartoon by Ruth Ahntholz in "Turning the Tables on Mormon Missionaries" January/February 1982.
Cartoon by bulbul in editorial March/April 1982. Cartoons by bulbul in Equal Pay columns, March/April 1982, March/April 1983, July/August 1983, and November/December 1983.
Photograph from The Brooklyn (NY) Museum of Arts of American and French Corsets in "Undercover Story Looks Beneath Surface," *New Directions for Women,* March/April 1983

ISBN: 978-1-59776-895-8
Library of Congress Cataloging-in-Publication Data: 2008940044

Kassell, Paula, 1917–
Taking women in new directions: Stories from the Second Wave of the Women's Movement. From New Directions for Women 1972–1993. The Issues That Galvanized Women to Change Society Completely & Forever.
By Paula Kassell

1.Feminism. 2. Women's rights. 3. Women-Social conditions. I. New directions for women. II. Title.

Manufactured in the United States of America

675 Dutchess Turnpike, Poughkeepsie, NY 12603
www.hudsonhousepub.com   (800) 724-1100

TABLE OF CONTENTS

Paula Kassell Always Took Women in New Directions

Preamble

vii	The price of equality is eternal persistence
viii	Introduction
x	This book is dedicated to
xi	And they said
xii	A College Girl Is Introduced to Margaret Mead (and Paula Kassell became a feminist) (Fall 1972)
xiii	Visiting Eleanor R. (Autumn 1979)
xiv	Tribute to Donna Allen (September 26, 1999)

Articles, Editorials and Book Reviews by Paula Kassell
in New Directions for Women

1	That Inexcusable 20 Percent (20% of the wage gap is due to discrimination) (editorial, Spring 1973)
2	Fewer Jobs for Women: *New Directions* to Research Reason (Summer 1973)
3	New Directions Continues Research (Winter 1974)
4	Editor Shakes Senate Hearing (about higher rate of women's joblessness) (Winter 1975)
5	Equal Rights: No Nonsense (Equal Rights Amendment) (editorial, Autumn 1975)
6	'Tragic Example' in Pennsylvania? (life under state ERA proves falsehood of lies told about ERA by opponents) (editorial, Summer 1976)
7	A Feminist Thinks About Prostitutes (Speak Up column, Autumn 1976)
8	Women's Famous Instigator (Book Review: *Going Too Far: The Personal Chronicle of a Feminist* by Robin Morgan, Winter 1977–78)
9	Zeroing in on Abortion Foes (first in series on national organizations) (Spring 1978)
10	NARAL-PAC Set to Oust Anti-Choice Congress Members (Spring 1978)
11	Priest Talks About Prostitutes (Autumn 1978)
13	Greece Seen Through New Eyes (Winter 1978–79)
15	The Painful Walk to Subjugation (shoe history and foot-binding in China) (Winter 1978–79)
17	Separate and Not Equal in the Workplace (job segregation and the pay gap) (Equal Pay column, Spring 1979)

18	Networks Needed (sharing information to document the pay gap) (Equal Pay column, Summer 1979)
19	Any Changes Ahead? (because men earn much more, women with jobs still doing housework, childcare and shopping, slowing change in sharing of chores) (Equal Pay column, January/February 1980)
20	Women Are Winning (job discrimination cases) (Equal Pay column, March/April 1980)
21	Brilliant—But Beautiful and Blonde (press frenzy over Mary Cunningham's friendship with her boss; ultimate ousting by the Bendix Corporation) (November/December 1980)
22	Media Still in Control of White Males (Equal Pay column, May/June 1981)
23	By Any Other Name (affirmative action) (Editorial, July/August 1981)
24	Equal Pay column (quotations about the family and housework, September/October 1981)
26	Nurses Assume New Militancy Over Pay (Equal Pay column, November/December 1981)
27	Turning the Tables on Mormon Missionaries (Speaking Personally, about the ERA, January/February 1982)
28	Open the Workplace to Women's Charities (Equal Pay column, January/February 1982)
29	Bad Swap! (moving Medicaid from states to federal government) (Editorial, March/April 1982)
30	Male Pride Equals Too Many Children (March/April 1982)
31	Family Photographs
36	Dad Sues NBC in Landmark Court Case (paternity leave for fathers) (Equal Pay column, March/April 1982)
37	Going Underground Has Its Pitfalls (coal mining) (Equal Pay column, May/June 1982)
38	Artist-Inventor-Activist Wrapped Up in One Suffragist (July/August 1982)
39	Child Care Ignored (Equal Pay column, July/August 1982)
40	Latch Key Children's Needs a Pressing Problem (Equal Pay column, September/October 1982)
41	Politicians Beware! (feminists more active in political campaigns) (Editorial, November/December 1982)
42	Hospitals May Fill Gap in Child Care (Equal Pay column, November/December 1982)
43	Discrimination in Marketplace a Reality (Equal Pay column, January/February 1983)
44	Unemployment Rates Deceiving (reasons for differences between women and men) (Equal Pay column, March/April 1983)
45	"Undercover Story" Looks Beneath Surface (corsets) (March/April 1983)
46	*In Defense of the Family: Raising Children in America Today* by **Rita Kramer** (Book Review, July/August 1983)

47	Brain Gender Gap: New Mythology (Book Review: *Sex and the Brain* by Jo Durden-Smith, September/October 1983)
48	*(The NY) Times'* Progress 'Woefully inadequate' (Equal Pay column, September/October 1983)
49	Names Will Never Hurt Us? (words we should never use) (Editorial, November/December 1983)
50	For Men Only (clubs that do not admit women) (March/April 1984)
52	What's a Wife Worth? Equal Pay column, May/June 1984
54	Affirmative Inaction (Reagan administration scuttles enforcement) (Editorial, July/August 1984)
55	Equal Pay column (sex segregation of jobs) (July/August 1984)
56	Equal Pay column (employment discrimination against women in Japan, clubs that do not admit women) (September/October 1984)
57	Ordeal by Press (as Geraldine Ferraro runs for Vice President) (Editorial, November/December 1984)
58	Hot Conference Holds Promise (history of the two United Nations Conferences on Women, looking forward to the third in Nairobi, Kenya in 1985) (International Roundup, July/August 1985)
59	Bitter Class Action Suit Against Church (Book Review: *Betrayal* by Merikay McLeod, September/October 1985)
60	New Feminism Examined (Book Review: *Controversy and Coalition: The New Feminist Movement* by Myra Marx Ferree and Beth B. Hess, September/October 1985)
61	Speaking Personally column (report on Women Gathering) (November/December 1985)
63	Facts Debunk Sociobiology (Book Review: *Myths of Gender: Biological Theories About Women and Men* by Anne Fausto-Sterling, July/August 1986)
64	Feminist Career Photographs
65	Miss . . . Mrs. . . . Ms. (how Paula Kassell induced *The New York Times* to use Ms.) (September/October 1986)
66	1986—Year of Red Herrings (examples of how the media distorts the feminist movement) (Editorial, January/February 1987)
67	Clothes Make the Woman (Smithsonian exhibition "Men and Women: A History of Costume, Gender and Power") (September/October 1990)
68	Nobody's Coming to Dinner Party (Judy Chicago's artwork kept from being exhibited) (November/December 1990)
69	Still Not the Newspaper It Should Be (Book Review: *The Girls in the Balcony: Women, Men and The New York Times* by Nan Robertson, March/April 1993)
70	Photo Lists

Appendix 1

72 **Sending Sons and Daughters Into Combat**
(*Daily Record*, **Morris County, N.J., April 5, 1987**)

73 **Dear Susan: ERA Still on Schedule** (*Daily Record*, **Morris County, N.J., February 15, 1989**)

74 **Letter to the editor of the** *Daily Record* **complaining about the headline (February 24, 1989)**

75 **Letter from the editor of the** *Daily Record* **in answer (March 13, 1989)**

Appendix 2

78 **Biography of Paula Kassell from** *Past and Present: Lives of New Jersey Women* **(1990) by Suzanne Messing**

81 **Paula Kassell Always Took Women in New Directions (Women's e-News Journalist of the Month, December 2003) by Betsy Wade**

83 **Feminist Activities of Paula Kassell**

Appendix 3

89 **The Birth, Success, Death and Lasting Influence of** *New Directions for Women* **(1972–1993 - ?)**

Appendix 4

97 **Acknowledgments**

Perhaps the most important lesson
The New York Times suit can teach us
Is that we may win a battle
But the war is unending.

The price of equality is eternal persistence.

INTRODUCTION

Martha Leslie Allen, Ph.D.
President, Women's Institute for Freedom of the Press

In the late 1960s, women-owned publications began sprouting up giving voice to the re-emerging women's movement. Paula Kassell was among the pioneers of this women's media movement that has continued to accelerate into the 21st century. Women need to retain a communication network of our own media in order to speak for ourselves. Without it, the male-owned media can portray us in inaccurate and stereotyped ways, and keep us excluded from news and from positions of power in government. Without our own media, there can be silence about issues vital to our lives such as violence against women. Without our own media, men can say our movement is dead and more people might believe them. Paula Kassell made sure that women's voices would be heard when she founded and ran *New Directions for Women,* which grew into a national newspaper with an ultimate circulation of 65,000.

Paula Kassell was an activist before she started her media work. In 1967, just a year after the National Organization for Women was founded, she joined. Her activism grew and continues to this day. She is a Vice President of the Women's Institute for Freedom of the Press and has played a leading role in the organization for decades.

The story of *New Directions for Women* and Kassell's role in it is an interesting one.

New Directions for Women grew out of the first statewide feminist conference held in New Jersey in April 1971, which Kassell suggested and coordinated. The need was discussed for a communication network to keep women in touch with each other both in and out of the women's movement. Kassell was given the responsibility for publishing the newspaper.

A detailed history of the paper's development is in the Appendix.

While Kassell and the other women worked to bring in money so the newspaper could grow, she was clear about her approach for women's media. "Our firm policy over the years we've been in business has been never to accept an ad for a product or service that we did not feel was good for our readers," Kassell stated in an interview in 1986. "Specifically, to use an example, we would never accept a cigarette ad, though we could probably make a lot of money from it because they would take a full page."

Kassell's work with *New Directions for Women* was a substantial contribution to the women's movement and to historians documenting the early years of the movement. But she made other significant contributions which impact women's lives.

One example is her successful effort to get the *New York Times* to use the honorific "Ms." in place of the maritally discriminatory "Miss" and "Mrs." On her own initiative, Kassell had bought 10 shares of Times stock solely to permit her to raise feminist issues in a well-reported forum, the annual *New York Times* shareholders meeting. Her raising the issue of titles in 1986 resulted in the paper finally capitulating. Kassell had for years been consulting with the women's caucus at *The Times* about strategy on this and other matters. She was great at both taking leadership herself and in working closely with others.

(See article titled "Miss..Mrs…Ms." which tells the true and complete story about why *The New York Times* was so recalcitrant in using "Ms." and how she induced *The Times* to start using it.)

Kassell decided not to add today's facts and figures after the articles because that would tie the book to its year of publication. The book is intended to illustrate historical situations as issues surfaced and the feminist movement developed over the 22 years that *New Directions for Women* was published. It will be relevant not only during the year of publication but far into the future. Students and researchers are encouraged to compare the prevailing facts as they use the book from year to year and decade to decade.

As well as guiding the newspaper from its founding, Kassell wrote on issues of concern to her and women throughout these years. It is exciting see her articles and editorials in print once again, so that, particularly in this age of paperless technology, we can sit down and read about the issues so dear to our hearts. It is a valuable part of our herstory and will allow historians to easily access these primary documents.

This book is dedicated to

Margaret Mead

Eleanor Roosevelt

Donna Allen

and

*Gerson Friedman,
my husband of 45 years,
the love of my life*

And *they said*

> Never doubt that
> A small group of thoughtful committed people
> can change the world. . . .
> Indeed, it's the only
> thing that ever has.
> 				Margaret Mead

> You must do the thing you think you cannot do.
> 				Eleanor Roosevelt

> Power is based on the number of people
> You can reach with your information.
> 				Donna Allen

> It's only money.
> 				Gerson Friedman

by the editor:

A College Girl Is Introduced to Margaret Mead

It's the story of the making of a feminist. It happened in 1935 when Margaret Mead published, "Sex and Temperament in Three Primitive Societies."

Three tribes on one island, New Guinea, each with a different way of bringing up its girls and boys, each producing women and men of different temperaments. The findings even surprised Margaret Mead.

"I concluded," she said, "that, until we could understand very thoroughly the way in which a society could mold all the men and women born within it to approximate an ideal of behavior which was congenial to only a few of them, or could limit to one sex an ideal of behavior which another culture succeeded in limiting to the opposite sex, we wouldn't be able to talk very intelligently about sex differences."

We're still not talking very intelligently about sex differences. But we are beginning to understand how socieities mold all women and men. And a few of us are struggling to escape the molds.

My struggle began when I read "Sex and Temperament in Three Primitive Societies." I must have been looking for help, because I was not comfortable in the mold called "woman" preparing for a woman's life in a man's world.

What a revelation to discover that our conception of the appropriate roles for female and male is not human nature, not inevitable. How else explain Mead's findings?

Here was one tribe in New Guinea, the Arapesh, whose girls and boys were both brought up to be gentle, cooperative—the men as well as the women devoted to caring for the children. Here was another tribe in New Guinea, just a few miles away, the Mundugamor, cannibals and head-hunters. Women and men both "expected to be violent, competitive, aggressively sexed, jealous and ready to see and avenge insult, delighting in display, in action, in fighting. The Mundugamor have selected as their ideal the very types of men and women which the Arapesh consider to be so incomprehensible that they hardly allow for their occurrence."

Sex Roles Reversed

Now consider the Tchambuli tribe, just another little distance across the jungle. The Arapesh and the Mundugamor give their women and men the same personality. The Tchambuli, like us, raise their girls and boys with personalities to complement each other. But it is the girls who are raised to be dominant and responsible. "As the women's task is to pay for the dance, the men's duty is to dance." A reversal of the way we are brought up!

Then I could escape! If society can make of us what it wills, then I could make of myself what I willed. I could be a woman interested in womanly things, but also interested in manly things (as those things are rigidly defined in our culture.)

Now Here We Are in 1972

Endless discussions go on today about whether militant feminists just want to be men. About whether women's lib is going to end up by making us all aggressive. About whether we are going to lose the better, warmer, nurturing qualities associated with womanhood while we try to gain the confidence and dominance associated with manhood.

Well, how should we go? We have the choice right now, when everything is changing rapidly. Can we control the change, change things for the better? What would it gain to change our ways if we all end up like violent, aggressive Mundugamors? What would it gain if women and men exchange roles? (There's already a book called "The Feminized Male.") I guess I would have been a happy Tchambuli, raised to be a dominant, independent responsible woman, because that's the way I turned out, and Western society does not make me very comfortable.

But, here I am in New Jersey, working toward a society that does not try to put anyone in a mold. I have a dream — a dream that some day each girl and boy can develop a personality and live a life built on her or his individual talents, aptitudes, intelligence and interests. I have a dream that we will stop molding our boys to be aggressive and willing to use violence. I have a hope that human beings free to be themselves will turn out to be like the Arapesh — gentle, cooperative and loving.

That is what I am living for since that day in 1935 when I was introduced to Margaret Mead.

Visiting Eleanor R.

Paula Kassell

Tears kept blurring my eyes as I studied the exhibits in the Eleanor Roosevelt wing of the museum at Hyde Park, N.Y. She headed my list of most-admired women when I was in college in the 30s, and no one has come close to deposing her, since.

This was a woman who thought she was ugly (her enemies agreed). She was so unsure of her self that she gratefully allowed Franklin's mother to rent and furnish their first home and supervise almost every detail of their family life. Married in 1905, she had five children by 1916. She was painfully shy until she overcame that to speak out after discovering primitive conditions while touring a Washington hospital during World War I, and was never silent again.

The final struggle for independence from her mother-in-law was made following Franklin's polio attack in 1921, after he was defeated as the Democratic candidate for vice president. His mother wanted him to retire to her home in Hyde Park, but Eleanor and Louis Howe, his mentor, urged him to increase his activities and stay in politics. He was elected governor of New York in 1928, served two-terms, and was inaugurated as president in 1933.

There is no doubt in my mind that the smartest decision Franklin ever made was to marry Eleanor. Eleanor also discovered that her position in the White House commanded the attention she needed to further her causes and influence the course of history.

The exhibits in the Eleanor Roosevelt wing gradually reveal every facet of her interests and character, even dozens of knitting needles, embroidery, and mending and darning paraphernalia. She is shown as she traveled throughout the country and the world, the eyes of her husband and the conscience of his presidency. The clothes she wore on these official visits have been preserved. There is a wool cape Franklin bought her in Scotland on their honeymoon — she used it all her life. There is the Red Cross uniform and cap she wore while visiting the troops overseas — it saved deciding what clothes to take, she said.

After her husband's death, President Truman appointed her to the United States delegation to the United Nations. As chair of the Human Rights Commission, she brought about, through her sensitive diplomacy, the adoption of the Universal Declaration of Human Rights in 1948. She had become the "First Lady of the World."

Visiting the Roosevelt home at Hyde Park showed an unexpected spartan side of Eleanor's nature — she used a small bedroom furnished only with a narrow bed with plain white coverlet, a small chest of drawers, a night-table and a chair. On either side of her room, with connecting doors, were Franklin's room and his mother's room, both large and comfortably furnished.

Her voice is perhaps the most haunting memory of the visit. She has recorded an Acoustiguide tour of the mansion. I remember her description of the huge living-room — the couch in front of one fireplace where she read to her young children after lunch, the two official high-backed chairs Franklin received as a two-term governor of New York, in front of the other fireplace. "Franklin always sat in the one on the left," she said in her warm, matter-of-fact voice, "and his mother always sat in the one on the right." Eleanor sits in my heart.

Donna Allen

Memorial September 26, 1999
By Paula Kassell

Donna and I started collaborating in 1972 and have been constant colleagues all these years. I coordinated or worked on most of the Women's Institute conferences. These were the face-to-face communication happenings that Donna called "dangerous" (to anti-feminists, that is) — letting feminists get together to air our mutual problems and to strategize. I remember particularly the Institute's Fourth Annual Conference on Planning a National and International Communications System for Women in 1982. Forty-seven women came from 30 countries, plus 73 women from 14 states of the United States. It was a hugely successful meeting with just about unanimous agreement on how to proceed globally. Since that long ago conference, those plans have come to fruition all over the world. The Institute's conferences were the most interesting and productive of all the feminist movement conferences I have attended. Donna was right.

Of all the excellent booklets the Institute has published to lay out programs and philosophy, the one that comes closest to my life as publisher and editor of New Directions for Women is "Power Is ... The Number of People You Can Reach With Your Information." Few people appreciate the truth and implications of that statement. The Institute's fostering and strengthening of feminist publications follows directly from that philosophy.

So far I have talked about the Women's Institute for Freedom of the Press more than about Donna. But the Institute IS Donna and Donna IS the Institute! Both are unique. I want to repeat here what I said about Donna when I introduced her to receive her medal as a Veteran Feminist of America in May. She leads an unusual life, one that enables her to accomplish the tremendous amount of work that she does. (I am unable to speak of Donna in the past tense; I must continue in present tense.) She goes to bed at 10:00 pm seven days a week, and gets up at 4:00 am and starts to work immediately; she gets a day's work done before the phones start ringing. All her meals are eaten at her desk — raw fruits and vegetables (no meat, no dairy). She never cooks. She takes a class in Ja Shin Do taught by her daughter Martha three times a week, where she has earned an orange belt (half way to a black belt). Donna has the most brilliant analytical mind of anyone I have ever met. So many times over the years and decades we have worked together I've drawn on her encyclopedic memory for media matters, especially about the impact of women's media.

Perhaps it might not be said that Donna is lovable; nevertheless I have come to love this old friend of mine. I can't imagine life without her. I have lost my best friend.

That Inexcusable 20 Percent

Do women earn less than men in the same jobs because they take time off for pregnancy and child-rearing while their male colleagues are progressing without interruption?

That question has been answered for the first time by the United States Department of Labor in a special report based on 1970 census information. Even after making allowances for the fact that women are more likely than men to work only part of the year or part-time; and even after allowing for the interruption of pregnancy, which does affect seniority and promotion progress — *even after making these allowances*, the Labor Department concluded that pay discrimination against women accounts for, *at a minimum*, 20 percent of the earnings gap. That answers the question right on the nail.

Let's look at an example. In the professional and technical fields, women's salaries are 48 percent of men's: men average $12,262 while their female *counterparts* average $5,927, a difference of $6,335. And 20 percent of $6,335 (that portion of the gap the Labor Department blames on sex discrimination) is $1,266.

No matter how you look at it, you are certainly not seeing equal pay for equal work.

Paula Kassell

Fewer Jobs for Women
New Directions to Research Reasons

Paula Kassell

Women in New Jersey consistently suffer a higher unemployment rate than men - in the first half of 1973, from 24 to 38 percent higher. The New Jersey Department of Labor and Industry compiles this data by sex at the request of New Directions for Women.

In May, unemployment among women reached 9 percent, up almost 1 percent since March. The May rate represents 105,000 unemployed women, up from 92,100 in March.

A spokesperson for the department attributed the higher rate partly to the preponderance of women in the apparel industry and electronic assembling. The rate in apparel is high, he said, because of the seasonal nature of the industry. And electronic companies have been severely cut back because of curtailment in defense spending.

Apparel union women blame imports for unemployment in American clothing plants. Connie department believes that seasonal fluctuations are smoothing out. She suggested that finding the reasons for women's high rate of unemployment is not easy. Many factors must be weighed - characteristics of employed women in general, rates for the skilled compared to the unskilled, for blacks compared to whites, for young workers compared to others.

New Directions for Women will continue to investigate the reasons for women's higher unemployment rates. Input from readers is welcome.

Robbie Cagnina, education coordinator of the International Union of Electrical Workers (IUE) District 3, also blamed imports and cited New Jersey plants that are phasing out and moving to foreign countries. The women who lose their jobs, many of them heads of families, cannot move into new jobs of other industries because they lack skills and education.

UNEMPLOYMENT IN NEW JERSEY Women's rate much higher than men's, month after month

Woodruff, of the International Ladies Garment Workers Union, pointed out that for many years union contracts have contained a "division of work" clause requiring employers to share the work when business is slack.

An authorized spokesperson in the Amalgamated research

To combat this, the IUE has an educational advancement program working through the locals to upgrade workers by on-the-job training - to learn how to operate new equipment, for instance. This program was federally funded until 1972. Now District 3 is carrying it alone.

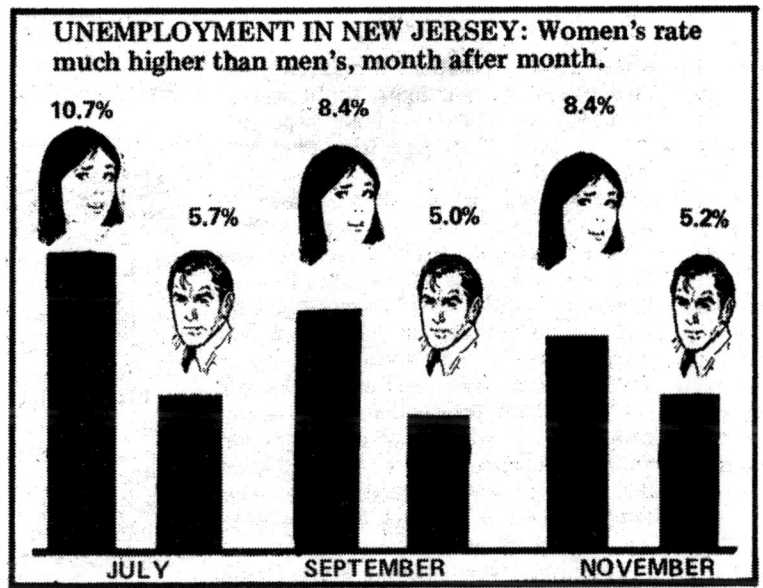

Fewer Jobs for Women
New Directions Continues Research

Paula Kassell

The unemployment rate for women in New Jersey continued high in the second half of 1973, much higher than the rate for men. In November, for instance, the latest month for which figures are available, 98,300 women were out of work. The rate for September was identical. And these months were about the best for women during the entire year.

Governor Byrne has ordered his new Commissioner of Labor and Industry, Joseph Hoffman, to tackle the state's high unemployment rate. Yet New Directions for Women has not found any responsible agency or researcher in or out of the government that is trying to find the causes behind so many unemployed women with a view to correcting them.

Herman C. Simonse, head of the Interdepartmental Committee on Economic Development, assured New Directions for Women in October 1973, that the committee was making a special effort to study women's unemployment, "along with other special groups such as minorities." In February 1974, Simonse reported that the committee has been preoccupied with studying the effects of the energy crisis on unemployment. They are now polling businesses in the state employing 1000 or more.

The New Jersey rates parallel national rates, but are higher, especially for women. The federal government is not coming up with answers to this disparity, either.

Instead they are working on a new method of collecting and reporting data that will become standard procedure in all states. As a result New Jersey data by sex will probably not be available until June 1974, according to John R. Sinton, Chief of Manpower Statistics and Analysis of the state's Department of Labor and Industry.

New Jersey unemployment rates might be lower under the new system, more in line with national rates, an analyst at the U.S. Bureau of Labor Statistics predicted. He attributed the expected reduction to more accurate techniques.

The women's rates, however, are expected to continue higher than the men's, nationwide and in New Jersey. And no one in New Jersey will know how much higher. Or the reasons. Or what to do about it.

Editor Shakes Senate Hearing

PAULA KASSELL

"Women are not working for pocket money," Paula Kassell, editor of **New Directions for Women in New Jersey**, told the U.S. Senate and Public Welfare Committee at its field hearings on unemployment in Passaic in mid-February. Her statistics on the high rate of jobless women - much higher than that for men - visibly shook Senator Harrison A. Williams (D-NJ), who chairs the committee.

In November 1973, the latest figures available, the statewide rate for out-of-work women was 8.4 percent while the men's rate was at 5.2 percent. Since that time the State Department of Labor and Industry discontinued the report it been preparing specifically for **New Directions for Women**.

Almost 42 percent of New Jersey women are in the labor force, according to Eileen Thorton, state president of the Women's Equity Action League, Kassell testified. "On the national level," she continued, "one out of ten women workers is a head of the household. Your committee cannot make plans to combat unemployment without knowing the head-of-household unemployment rate by sex," she told Senator Williams.

"It is important to consider that 42 percent of working men do not have husbands to support them," she declared, "because 23 percent of working women are single and 19 percent are widowed, divorced or separated. Another 18.9 percent of working women have husbands with incomes under $7,000 a year.

Kassell cautioned against thinking that married women take jobs from men. "In fact, most unemployed men do not have the education or skills to qualify for most of the jobs held by women. Chaos would result in business, industry, services and government if women quit their jobs," she said.

"Not looking at the full picture regarding women - such a large part of New Jersey's unemployed labor force - is trying to plan in the dark," Kassell said. "For instance, spurring home and highway construction will not open jobs to women because they are systematically excluded from the trades."

Kassell recommended that the committee study a pilot trade apprenticeship program in Wisconsin. Their survey found

(continued on page 10)

(continued from page 1)

women's dropout rate was half that for men. There was a high degree of employer satisfaction with women apprentices.

"Governments on all levels are economizing by reducing funds for social services, hospital care, mental health, child care centers, and training for the retarded and handicapped. This not only harms the unfortunate people who need the services - it also puts more women out of work because these are traditionally women's jobs," Kassell stressed.

"Some day," she told Senator Williams, "but not in our time, sex discrimination will be completely eliminated, and it will not be necessary to study the economic problems of women. But the laws against job discrimination are not being enforced, and you have to face the realities of the situation in trying to get women back to work today."

Equal Rights — no nonsense

In November the voters of New Jersey will be asked to ratify— or reject—the Equal Rights Amendment to the state consitution, guaranteeing that "equality of rights under law shall not be abridged on account of sex."

We have been bombarded with nonsense about what this law means. It does not concern itself with integrating toilet facilities, dormitories and hospital rooms, or forcing churches to ordain women priests. Claiming that all these things will be required if the amendment is passed insults the intelligence of our voters.

The amendment will only make unconstitutional any law—state, county or municipal—that discriminates against either sex. Can our voters be made to believe that lawmakers are going to sit in solemn session and pass laws that the sexes must go to the toilet together? The Supreme Court has already ruled to protect personal privacy: no law could take that privilege away.

Nor will the amendment prevent women from being awarded alimony or child-support— the courts are already deciding each case according to each family's situation and will continue to do so whether or not the Equal Rights Amendment is passed.

Nor will the amendment require that every wife be self-supporting or child-supporting. No law now interferes with each family's right to decide who stays home and who works. Can our voters be made to believe that lawmakers are going to pass laws requiring that every individual adult go to work and be self-supporting or that every child must be placed in a child-care center?

Nor will this amendment to the state constitution make women subject to the draft, because New Jersey does not have an army or the power to draft soldiers. But scare tactics about military service are being used to confuse the state and federal amendments, so we are compelled to discuss the issue on its merits.

Yes, an Equal Rights Amendment to the federal constitution would make women equally subject to the draft and equally governed by its exemptions and deferments. It is terrible to imagine our daughters going to war — but aren't our sons just as precious to us? Centuries of warfare have unfortunately accustomed us to losing our sons, while our school books have lost the history of women's military exploits. And down the years we and our daughters have never escaped being ravaged by the wars that men have made. On the practical side, because of discriminatory military admissions policies, all but a very few of our daughters are now deprived of veteran's benefits and privileges, and the training and education that military service provides.

The opposition has no name. It also has no truthful, factual reasons to vote against the Equal Rights Amendment. If it did—if there were important reasons to vote against the amendment—would we be hearing over and over again about those integrated toilets?

Paula Kassell

'Tragic example' in Pennsylvania?

Women traveling in Pennsylvania to celebrate our nation's history (see story about Philadelphia's Bicentennial Women's Center and Feminist Tours in this issue) will have a fine opportunity to see for themselves what life will be like after the Equal Rights Amendment (ERA) is added to the Constitution.

Pennsylvania passed a state Equal Rights Amendment five years ago, in May 1971. None of the awful consequences have occurred that were predicted by the opponents of equal rights for all Americans:

- The right to privacy has not been challenged. Travelers will find that separate restroom facilities are still maintained.
- Mothers have not been forced to go to work to contribute half the support of their children. The court decision on this issue (Green v. Freiheit) reads "... the duty of child support no longer rests primarily with the father, but must be divided between the parents according to their ability to pay. This is not, of course, to suggest that a mother who is keeping a house and caring for her children must secure the services of a baby sitter and seek employment in order to contribute to the children's financial support; it is obvious that a mother who is caring for her children is providing them with valuable support."
- Passage of the ERA is not responsible for placing separated and divorced women unwillingly in the work force. In awarding alimony and support and in property settlements, the courts are maintaining that relative financial position, earning capacity and needs must be taken into account.
- The Equal Rights Amendment has not caused the demise of the family in Pennsylvania. The divorce rate is about half the national average.
- Same-sex marriages have not been legalized.

Stop-ERA is not telling the truth about what has happened in Pennsylvania since 1971. Their literature calls Pennsylvania a "tragic example" of a state overrun with "unisex" public toilets and plagued by homosexual marriages. Millions of people traveling in the state this bicentennial year will have the opportunity to use public toilets, to talk to Pennsylvanians, especially the wives and mothers — and to find out the truth for themselves.

Then they can come home and ask the people who oppose equal rights: Why are you misinforming the voters? Why are you threatening women with having to go to work, married or not? Why are you telling women they will not be able to receive alimony or child support? When none of this is true.

They can ask the leaders of the fight against equal rights: Who is benefiting by these falsehoods? Who is providing the money to print millions of leaflets to spread these falsehoods? To bus hundreds of people to demonstrations?

THE AMERICAN PEOPLE ARE ENTITLED TO KNOW THE WHOLE TRUTH.

Paula Kassell

Speak Up

A feminist thinks about prostitutes

I can't make up my mind about prostitutes. Ever since the mid-1960s, when I became active as a feminist, I have been trying to develop an attitude or philosophy about the profession that squares with my deep commitment to individual freedom of choice for all women.

- *On the one hand, why not look upon it as a very well paying, not too demanding, way of earning a living?*

But I cringe when I imagine a woman opening herself to this most intimate act with any stranger who wants to rent her body.

- *On the one hand, there are women who endure distasteful marriages year after year. Legally and by still universally accepted custom, a husband has access to his wife's body, figuratively if not literally, on demand—rape laws consistently exempt husbands. In a real sense, these wives are selling their sexual services, perhaps because they are not equipped to support themselves in the manner to which they are accustomed.*

But one of the marvelous aspects of the women's movement has been recognition of woman as a sexual being—we are liberated to enjoy sex, to choose to participate as equals, to be assured satisfaction. Not too long ago (only one generation), it was a horrifying thought to imagine that a woman could enjoy the sex act or be capable of orgasm. Now women are known to have strong sex appetites and capabilities even beyond men's.

- *On the one hand, why is prostitution, this "victimless crime," considered a crime at all?*

But isn't the prostitute the victim of her pimp? (This is a relationship I cannot fathom.) And isn't the prostitute often used to set up her customer for robbery?

And so goes my thinking about prostitution: pro and con, modern and traditional. There is no feminist position. Should there be? Yes, for two reasons—one practical and timely, the other philosophical and of the future.

Laws against prostitution and their enforcement discriminate against and harass women every day, usually leaving the male customers scot free. The courts and prosecuting officials are leaning toward eliminating laws against prostitution and the graft they foster. Society as a whole (and women in particular) has more to gain by legally ignoring prostitution than trying to outlaw it (which has not succeeded in thousands of years.

Looking ahead far into the future, when women's battle for complete equality is won, prostitution will disappear—society's customs and the relations between the sexes will be so radically different that sex for hire will seem like a quaint ancient custom. Buying and selling the use of a woman's body will be as outdated as slavery.

So prostitution as an entrenched feature of our present society must become a feminist issue. No woman should feel so far removed from it that she need not face thinking about its implications, trying to understand it. Because the widespread practice of buying and selling women's bodies is a true reflection of the status of women.

Paula Kassell

Women's famous instigator

GOING TOO FAR: THE PERSONAL CHRONICLE OF A FEMINIST by Robin Morgan (Random House) $10.00

Paula Kassell

Robin Morgan: a name written right after Betty Friedan's in the consciousness-raising years of the late 1960s and early 1970s. She was the editor of SISTERHOOD IS POWERFUL: An Anthology of Writings from the Women's Liberation Movement, and we will never outlive its effect on us. Now GOING TOO FAR takes us behind those scenes of our history with one who made it.

She shares everything with us—her private letters, her love for her husband and the problems of the marriage, her uncertainties and second thoughts. What a vulnerable person she has been, and she pressed on regardless. Most relevant to us today, she experienced and recorded the coming together of hundreds of diverse women who found sisterhood.

It would have been worth while just to have so many of her articles in one place. But the real value of the book lies in the introductions she has written for each piece. "I found a dialogue emerging between my voice today and my voice at the time of the piece's writing," she says. In the preface she characterizes her writings as "map notations in the journey of an individual woman through uncharted territory, via the intertwined roads of daughterhood, artistry, marriage, motherhood, radicalism."

Because she was "in on" or indeed an instigator of so many of the famous events of the women's movement, we learn, for the first time perhaps, what REALLY happened when women disrupted the Miss America pageant in 1968 and how the false story of "bra burning" was invented. We learn how and why the women in the radical left movement seized control of Rat, a major underground newspaper. Her article, "Goodbye to All That," written for the women's first issue, tells for all time why women cannot hope for their own liberation and rights as a result of (reward for?) their hard work for the rights of others or even for human rights. Women's rights are not necessarily included—the treatment of radical left women in the 1970s paralleled the treatment of women in the 1860s who worked to free and enfranchise the slaves. "We have met the enemy and he is our friend," is her insight.

It was a delicious experience to read "WITCH Hexes Wall Street" (Halloween, 1968), "WITCH at the Counter-Inaugural Ball" (first inauguration of Richard Nixon, January 1969), "WITCH Hexes the Bridal Fair" (first New York Bridal Fair, Madison Square Garden, 1969—they released 150 live white mice at the trousseau fashion show, and that was only one of the actions). WITCH stands for Women's International Terrorist Conspiracy from Hell, a child of New York Radical Women.

Those of us who took part in or were awakened by the feminist actions of the last two decades know Robin Morgan's place in our eventful history and our literary history. Yet in characteristic modesty she has omitted **Sisterhood Is Powerful** from the long Germinal Reading List included in the new book. That is going too far!

Zeroing in on abortion foes

This is the first in a series on the important national organizations working for women's equality and advancement. Future articles will tell what every woman needs to know about NOW (National Organization for Women), WEAL (Women's Equity Action League), Women's Lobby, Women's Campaign Fund, ERAmerica and others listed in the directory elsewhere in this issue.

Paula Kassell

ABORTION ILLEGAL — ANNUAL DEATH TOLL IN THOUSANDS PREDICTED. LEGISLATOR'S DAUGHTER'S SUICIDE LINKED TO ABORTION BAN. WOMEN FIND CLINIC PADLOCKED. These are some of the headlines in a mock newspaper — dateline: "Someday Soon" — produced by NARAL to dramatize our future if women lose the right to legal abortion.

NARAL is the only national membership and lobbying organization with the single purpose of keeping abortion safe and legal. Started in 1969 as the National Association for the Repeal of Abortion Laws, it became the National Abortion Rights Action League after the triumph of the 1973 Supreme Court decision, and now has affiliates in almost every state.

In 1973, the Court recognized the right to abortion as constitutionally guaranteed and ruled that the decision should be between a woman and her physician.

In 1974, according to NARAL, 900,000 women had legal, medically safe abortions; 300,000 of them were teenagers. Over 1 million women had legal abortions in 1976. But it is believed that over a half-million additional women needed abortion services in 1976 and were not able to obtain them. Most public hospitals are not providing abortions (only 18 percent do, in fact).

Then, in June 1977, the Supreme Court ruled that neither the Constitution nor federal law required states to spend Medicaid funds for elective abortions. It also held that public hospitals need not support or permit them.

And in August, the Court upheld the Hyde amendment to the Labor-HEW funding bill, and federal Medicaid funds were cut off. An estimated 250,000 to 300,000 women received government-financed abortions annually prior to this cut-off. Today only a few states continue to pay for Medicaid abortions without federal help.

Writing for the majority in the June Medicaid cut-off case, Supreme Court Justice Lewis Powell held that a state "has a valid and important interest in encouraging childbirth." Karen Mulhauser, NARAL's executive director, says their research has turned up no legislation or court cases in our history to document that interest. "It's something that came out of Justice Powell's head," she concluded. "If the state can take the right to an abortion away from a woman who depends on Medicaid, is this not a precedent for the state to take away all women's rights to choose an abortion, even if they can afford it, because of the superiority of the state's interest in childbearing?" Mulhauser asked in a public hearing. "And given the variety of other birth control programs supported by the states and the federal government, why should the state choose only this one to deny respect for persons because of the newly discovered 'state's interest in childbearing'?" she continued.

Representative Henry Hyde, whose amendment was upheld by the Court, is quoted by NARAL as expaining his motivation thus: "I certainly would like to prevent, if I could legally, anybody having an abortion, a rich woman, a middle-class woman, or a poor woman. Unfortunately, the only vehicle available is the HEW Medicaid bill."

NARAL-PAC set to oust anti-choice Congress members

Working against NARAL toward that total ban are a number of hardhitting well-funded organizations. NARAL monitors the money raised by the anti-abortion movement and reports that one of them, the National Committee for Human Life Amendment, raised $906,404 from January 1976 to March 1977 alone, about half of it in contributions of $500 and more.

To compete, NARAL conducts a never ending campaign for members and contributions. A large ad that ran in The New York Times of October 23, 1977, quoted Hyde, Stennis and other anti-choice members of Congress, and was headlined, "We're Mad." The ad ended with a space for readers to write a letter that NARAL would deliver to Congress.

Hoping to rid Congress of such members, NARAL last October formed a political action committee, NARAL-PAC, to raise funds

---

"I certainly would like to prevent, if I could legally, anybody having an abortion, a rich woman, a middle-class woman, or a poor woman. Unfortunately, the only vehicle available is the HEW Medicaid bill."

Representative Henry Hyde

---

for pro-choice candidates in the 1978 congressional campaigns. Betsy Shotin has been named director.

We have "tried for years to appeal to elected officials with rational arguments. And for years these same elected officials have refused to view women's right to choose as a medical or human rights issue. It is now clear that the pro-choice majority must be mobilized to get out and vote for pro-choice candidates," NARAL explained in its announcement. Grassroots organizing will be its major new focus in 1978. "We hope to raise $100,000 to spend on a few important targeted races," said Mulhauser. "A contribution to NARAL-PAC is tax-deductible up to $100 if no other campaign contribution has been made in the calendar year. An individual can contribute up to $5,000 to NARAL-PAC in each calendar year."

Asked if NARAL-PAC was formed in reaction to the recent decision by the Women's Campaign Fund to consider funding women candidates who were not necessarily pro-choice, Mulhauser pointed out that NARAL-PAC will be free to fund men as well as women and will campaign against anti-abortion candidates in addition to supporting pro-choice candidates. She expects abortion rights to be a major issue in 1978.

NARAL's imaginative brochures and promotional mailings combine rational, informational contents with the hard sock to the emotions it hopes will shock women into taking action to recoup our recent losses and stave off the threats to our legal right to have an abortion.

For further information or to contribute to NARAL or NARAL-PAC: National Abortion Rights Action League, 825 15 St., NW, Washington, DC 20005 (202) 347-7774.

Priest talks about prostitutes

Paula Kassell

I have been pondering prostitution as a feminist issue ever since the mid-1960s, when I first became active in the women's movement (see "A feminist thinks about prostitutes," Autumn 1976). There is no doubt in my mind that it is a feminist issue, because the widespread practice of buying and selling the use of women's bodies is a true reflection of the status of women.

The National Organization for Women and other women's groups support decriminalization of prostitution — that is, repeal of all laws making prostitution a crime. And feminists in New York City walked the streets in a "loiter-in" for a few nights, risking arrest to protest the law against loitering for solicitation that was hurriedly passed to sanitize the city for the 1976 national Democratic convention.

But when I looked for a feminist in close contact with street prostitutes, I found only Depaul Genska, a Catholic priest of the Franciscan order.

For six years, since a chance meeting with two street women on Lexington Avenue, he has spent a few nights a week in New York City befriending prostitutes, helping just by being available — to take them to dinner, baby-sit with their children, or whatever. Occasionally he is able to assist a woman who wants to leave "the life" with temporary funds, a place to stay, perhaps a job. But he emphasizes that he is not trying to bring religion or teach morality, only to be a human resource.

So I asked him how prostitutes and "straight" or "square" women (as non-prostitutes are called in the trade) are or are not relating to each other, and this led to a wide-ranging discussion.

Paula Kassell: Is there a feeling of sisterhood?

DePaul Genska: No. The prostitute feels threatened by anybody in the "square" community. She sees a "square woman," a "married woman." The adjective gets in the way. She may feel a little more bonding with women in the women's movement because feminists have a reputation for openness to other lifestyles.

But my impression regarding women in the women's movement is that they do not understand that some women want to be prostitutes, and their reaction is, "How can any woman do that?"

PK: Are prostitutes organized to help each other?

DG: No. Prostitutes as a group is fiction. They are in competition with each other. Margo St. James' COYOTE is one exception. Scapegoat, run by Mari Maggu, who left "the life" after 12 years, is another. She helps street women in New York City get medical attention, legal services, child care and food stamps.

Street women are so harassed by society that they are intimidated even to go to a doctor's office for an examination. And, in fact, doctors do exploit these women for sexual services as soon as they find out they are prostitutes. Any situation you can think of where women have been hassled, the prostitute gets it tenfold. Square society cannot think of her as a normal human being.

Any situation you can think of where women have been hassled, the prostitute gets it tenfold. She is literally up for grabs.

PK: Is the sexual revolution decreasing the demand for prostitutes now that more and more people are doing it for nothing and at younger and younger ages?

DG: No. Demand is going higher. It is more intriguing to do something that's forbidden. Taking the laws away might defuse the bomb. Even the prostitute has the psychology of defiance of the law. Mari Maggu was arrested 1,536 times. Another reason is "kinky" sex — sex acts that most men would not ask their dates or wives to do. Men also feel safer as anonymous "Johns" instead of taking a chance with a neighbor or coworker who might tell.

PK: Is it true that prostitutes are involved in robbing their customers?

DG: Yes. For instance, 15 to 20 percent of the crimes reported in the Times Square area are prostitute-related. And there must be hundreds of men who do not even report being robbed while patronizing a prostitute. Rolling and robbing customers increase after police raids — the pimps demand their money even though their women have been arrested and have paid large fines.

Bill Barrett

Depaul Genska

I have come to the conclusion myself — very firmly so — that prostitution is going to happen. So let it happen under the best of circumstances. Try to make it more humane for the people who are in it. We take prostitution too seriously and try to stamp it out, and don't take prostitutes seriously enough. We don't respect the rights of the women (for housing, for instance) and their problems in raising their children.

At least 7 million people are involved in prostitution. It has been estimated by the criminal justice system that there are 500,000 prostitutes in the United States, and this does not include the call girls, who rarely tangle with the law. Add to that number customers, pimps, children — 80 to 90 percent of prostitutes have children — and the total might perhaps be double 7 million.

A favorite trick of pimps is to demand custody of the children and farm them out to his relatives, in the south, perhaps. If the mother ever wants to leave him or the life, he has a stranglehold on her; he threatens that she will never see her children again; she may not even know where they are.

PK:...Prostitutes must try to reach other women. Mari Maggu, for instance, who publicly identifies herself as an ex'prostitute and is working in an organization for prostitutes, has to take it upon herself to go out and meet the feminists and ask them to help prostitutes — tell them that decriminalization is very important, tell them why legalization is bad. Otherwise we will never understand prostitutes or their problems. Margo St. James is the only one I know of who is reaching feminists.

DG: Margo is unusual. She has learned to operate in the real world. If somebody like Mari Maggu came to a meeting, she would want a resolution passed immediately. She could not tolerate the aggravation of parliamentary procedure, amendments, discussion, worrying, "Will it pass?" That takes a lot of time and effort for which she sees little or no monetary return.

PK:...The reward has to come in educating women.

DG: Yes, but prostitutes are practical women. Decriminalization hasn't a chance in the world right now, or soon.

Greece seen through new eyes

Paula Kassell

Women in Greece are living the same lives as their great-great-grandmothers, rising before dawn to take the sheep to pasture, hand-weaving rugs for their daughters' dowries, unable to read and write.

Women in Greece are successful lawyers, doctors, engineers and architects, and members of parliament. There is no discrimination against women's admittance to universities and professional schools because it is based on competitive examinations.

Both statements are true. In the interior villages, life has not changed. In Athens, life is as modern and fast paced as New York's.

In September I toured Greece with the Women's Union of Greece, together with women invited from the U.S., Canada, England, Norway, Sweden, Australia and Japan (and a few of their husbands).

We visited the ancient sites and the islands and swam in the navy blue waters of the Aegean Sea. But what was more important to me were the bus trips into small villages and cities in the mountainous interior that tourists seldom see. We talked with many women through the excellent interpretive skills of the Women's Union members.

Four women members of parliament conducted seminars about politics, employment discrimination, family planning and legislation (see interview with Melina Mercouri). There are 11 women in the Greek parliament out of a total membership of 300, almost exactly the same ratio as in the U.S. House of Representatives.

The Women's Union was organized three years ago by women active in the Panhellenic Socialist Party out of the conviction that women themselves must define and work for the changes they need. For that reason the union is outside the party and actively recruiting non-socialist women to membership. Its two-fold motto is: "There can be no women's liberation without social liberation. There can be no social liberation without women's liberation."

Its general aims are not only to enlighten women "on the nature and source of their oppression" and organize women to "struggle for equal participation with men" but also to attack "everyday problems in order to reach a better and more socially just world." The immediate goals are: child care centers, fighting illiteracy, medical and legal counseling centers, protection of Greek culture, protection of the aged, protection of the environment.

Margaret Papandreou, vice president of the Women's Union, is an American-born woman married to Andreas Papandreou, head of the Socialist Party. She and her husband both believe that working for women's issues will prove to be good for the party, she told me. "But if conflicts occur, I will just have to face them and stand up for what I believe in," she declared.

The founder of the Women's Union, Kakia Genimata, was also a founder of the Panhellenic Socialist Party. When I asked her what influences in her life account for her leadership and determination, she answered, "Nothing!" This is a more perceptive answer than it seems. These women find their strengths within their own experiences and awareness. Genimata no longer wants a leadership role within the

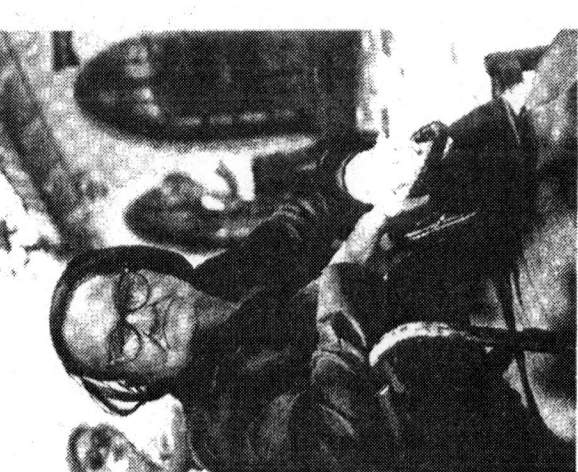
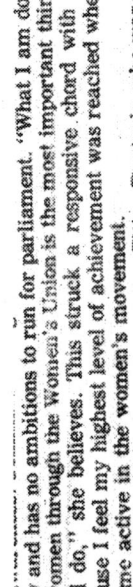

party and has no ambitions to run for parliament. "What I am doing for women through the Women's Union is the most important thing I could do," she believes. This struck a responsive chord with me because I feel my highest level of achievement was reached when I became active in the women's movement.

But there is another young woman, Ttitna Pantazis, who was imprisoned and tortured by the military junta that controlled Greece from 1967 to 1974. Her abilities and enthusiasm shine through undimmed, even when she is only interpreting for a village woman. She outlined for us the Women's Union program for combating the problems of the agricultural woman: pensions, education, cultural and informational meetings, hospitals, for instance. This is a woman who belongs in parliament implementing these goals, so that Anna Barka's daughters will not need to lead her life.

Anna Barka lives in the 300-family agricultural village of Karies, near the city of Yannena in central Greece. The area is mountainous and arid. She went over her daily schedule for me:

4:00 a.m. Wake up.

Morning chores. Feed the family. Get the children ready for school. With husband, take their sheep very far out of the village to the free pasture land owned by the government (nearby land is owned by the church, which charges rent). Return to the village, take the mule down to the valley to cultivate their fields and pick vegetables for the evening meal.

Afternoon chores. Clean the house. Wash clothes (by hand). Cook the evening meal.

Evening chores. Weave or sew for her daughters' dowries (using traditional Greek crafts).

10:00 p.m. Go to bed.

The women in their teens or early 20s vigorously deny that they will lead the lives of their mothers. Since village life offers no options they are leaving for the cities. One of the young women said she wishes a factory would come to Karies so that she can find work and earn a pension.

It was not always thus for women in Greece. The village of Monadendri, whose population is now down to 90, was once a prosperous matriarchy. From the mid-1400s to the mid-1800s, women were educated and they administered large estates. The first high school for girls in Greece was opened in Monadendra about 1700.

Building on this tradition, when in 1940 the Italian army invaded Greece near Monadendri (which is near the Albanian border), the women of the village carried ammunition and machine guns over the mountains to the Greek army, even in winter.

Though Greek women have century after century martyred themselves in wartime (against the Turks, for instance, who occupied the country for 400 years), they have achieved no political significance and are still kept isolated from decision-making.

Nevertheless, in 1975 a law requiring equal pay for work of equal value was enacted, becoming effective in June 1978. But, we were told, employers are already transferring women from job to job to prevent them from becoming qualified for advancement.

And though education is compulsory until age 16, girls under 14 can be employed so long as they have a relative working in the same industry. Forty-four percent of the women are completely illiterate or have attended only early elementary grades.

That presents one of the problems that faces the Women's Union. How are these women to be reached?

The answer is "simplicity," said Elpida Praxiadou, who heads the Provinces Committee of the Women's Union. They enter a village and, going door-to-door, ask the women about their lives and discuss their problems. They find that women are working 20 hours a day, isolated, with no newspapers, receiving none of the information they need. But they see change coming. "One generation ago, women started to work outside the home, and that was the beginning," Praxiadou said. "This generation struggles, and mothers find it hard to understand what the young women of today want."

The Provinces Committee aims gradually to form a Women's Union chapter in every village. Some day, they hope, they will be organized to teach the women to read and write, for there is little chance of government interest.

Contraceptives, abortion and sterilization are illegal in Greece. But Dr. Marie Pareikas, a physician who is also a member of parliament, is hopeful that this will soon be changed. The Socialist Party has succeeded in attaching a decree legalizing abortion to a law regarding the transplantation of organs that is about to be introduced in parliament, she told us. In the meantime, doctors prescribe the Pill, IUDs and other contraceptives for "therapeutic" reasons. Pharmacies also supply the Pill without prescription, in defiance of the law. The anti-abortion bill is harsh—the woman, the doctor and even the woman's escort can be jailed, and the doctor can be barred from practicing medicine. Yet "thousands of abortions take place," Dr. Pareikas said, and Greece has an extremely low birth-rate.

Opponents of legalization cite underpopulation. "If we go on as we are now, in the year 2,000 there will be 80 million Turks and only 12 million Greeks," explained Professor Andreas Gazis, who headed a commission to draft new legislation.

Greece adopted a new constitution in 1975 that gives men and women equal rights and responsibilities, but this clause will not go into effect until 1982.

As Greek family law now stands, the man is head of the household and the wife must take his name (but professional women use their own names professionally). The mother has no legal rights over her children while the father is alive. Even after his death, the children are under the guardianship of an advisor previously appointed by her husband.

Dowries for daughters are obligatory. Under civil law, the woman retains ownership of the dowry, but her husband controls it and retains the income. Upon divorce, the woman takes back the dowry. The Women's Union is demanding abolition of the dowry. It is such a financial burden on the family that the birth of a daughter is considered a calamity.

Even Sue Androniou, the energetic young lawyer who conducted the symposium on family law, accepted a dowry from her father—ownership of an apartment in Athens for which her family had been saving since she was born. However, before deciding to marry, she made sure that her fiance renounced a dowry as a condition for marriage, and both of them are trying to live their family life as equals.

The traditions are crumbling.

To know these Greek women and to visit Greece's archaeological sites in their company is to understand the people who gave the west its ancient heritage of philosophy, beauty and democracy. These women can give Greece its new heritage.

The painful walk to subjugation

Paula Kassell

Fashion has distorted the human body from head but not to toe since primitive times. Only in high civilizations do we find injurious shoes. Like American Indian moccasins, the shoes of primitive peoples and, even today, the shoes of undeveloped nations are flat and conform to the natural foot.

This was strikingly demonstrated at The Great American Foot exhibit of the Museum of Contemporary Crafts which opened in New York last spring and is now on a national tour (see itinerary). The title is a misnomer, since the show included shoes worn through the ages all over the world.

"In an average lifetime, our feet carry us over 65,000 miles, more than two and a half times around the world! Composed of 26 bones, 107 ligaments, and 19 muscles, the foot has for centuries nurtured custom, incited superstition, influenced fashion ...," wrote Ruth Amdur Tanenhous, exhibition curator, in the show catalog.

But not just any foot. The male foot has, with few exceptions, been well shod over the centuries. It is the female foot that has inspired myths, causing it to be used for purposes far removed from — in fact inimical to — carrying the female body from place to place.

The brutal subjugation of Chinese women through footbinding comes instantly to mind. This custom started in the 10th century and continued until after it was outlawed in 1912. Travelers in the Chinese countryside can still see bound feet among elderly women.

Starting usually at the age of five or six but sometimes as early as age three, girls' four small toes were broken and bent under the sole, and the sole and heel were forged as close together as possible. The ideal product was a "three-inch golden lotus." Women in the upper class had to be carried on palanquins. Women in the lower class were forced to hobble about on short stumps. The result was great pain and suffering for 60 to 80 percent of the female population. It was said that one out of ten girls died from footbinding or its after effects — severed tendons, ulcers, blood poisoning.

The process and purposes are described by Susan Greenhalgh in "Bound Feet, Hobbled Lives: Women in Old China" for Frontiers: A Journal of Women's Studies. "Lovers were infatuated by a foot peeking out from the coverlet. Lascivious men even claimed that binding forced the blood to flow upward, increasing the development of the buttocks and thighs, and enhancing the voluptuousness of the vagina."

The real reasons were economic and patriarchal. Though it started in the court of a 10th century T'ang Dynasty emperor, footbinding gradually spread to women in all segments of society. Upper class families picked it up as testimony that they could afford to support crippled women. The sooner, the tighter and the tinier the feet were bound, the more conspicuously wasteful the family proved itself to be. Then lower class families hoping to marry daughters into richer families bound their feet.

But the conspicuous leisure theory is not enough. The greatest threat to the family system in China came from women, because they married in from an outside family, says Greenhalgh. With footbinding the patriarchal family had a superb device for physically preventing the women from disrupting its stability. Unable to wander far or do any labor, the young wife was confined to her husband's home. Once footbinding was established, Greenhalgh concludes, its perpetuation became bound up with that of the family system in a vicious, self-repetitive cycle.

The myth of tiny female feet is not confined to China and times past. In his book, "The Unfashionable Human Body," Bernard Rudofsky examines the Cinderella story with a sympathetic glance at the two sisters with large feet. "The tale of Cinderella, a veritable case history from the psychopathology of dress," he points out, "has its protagonists made to order for the couch: The august shoe fetishist who turns the country upside down to satisfy his craving for a miniature foot; the maniacal mother with the instincts of a procuress and the tenderness of a hangman; and the unappreciated heroines of the story — obedient daughters and true martyrs in the cause of sartorial perfection — whose keepsakes from the sleaziest of all love affairs are mangled feet.

The Great American Foot
Exhibit Itinerary

Junior Arts Center, Los Angeles — Now through Dec. 5
Downtown Center, Fine Arts Museums, San Francisco — Jan. 28–Mar. 4, 1979
Bellevue Art Museum, Bellevue, Wash. — Apr. 6–May 12, 1979
Milwaukee Art Center. Milwaukee — July 1–Aug. 5, 1979
Joel Evans Appalachian Center for Crafts, Smithville, Tenn. — Sep. 9–Oct. 13, 1979
Brunnier Gallery, Iowa State University, Ames, Iowa — Oct. 30–Dec. 4, 1979

The exhibit is organized by the Museum of Contemporary Crafts of the American Crafts Council, 44 West 53 St., New York, N.Y. 10019.

"Even the bowdlerized versions of Cinderella cannot fail to impress children with the fact that the choice of the sovereign princess depended on her shoe size."

And then there is the chopine, popular for centuries, notably in France, Italy, Turkey and Japan. This was a shoe built on a high, narrow platform; in 15th century Venice it reached a height of 20 (twenty!) inches. The chopine was of "singular momentousness" in costume history, according to Rudofsky. It "was instrumental in changing the proportion, posture and gait of a woman," he explains. "Until then, men and women had been, literally, on equal footing...their carriage had remained fairly natural ... Chopines were the instrument and symbol of woman's submission to man... the sight of a woman walking precariously closely corresponded to man's image of feminine helplessness. The sex appeal of an unnatural walk persists," Rudofsky notes.

Women are still willingly paying a terrible price for that sex appeal, especially when it depends on pointed toes and high heels. Dr. Benjamin Kauth, a podiatrist on the Public Information Committee of the American Podiatry Association, sometimes has to operate on women for a pinched nerve just behind the toes, caused by wearing pointed-toe shoes. The condition, causing sharp pain, is very common, Dr. Kauth said.

Four-inch heels are popular in 1978 shoe fashions, although even on three-inch heels "all the internal organs are compressed," according to Dr. Kauth. And that's not all. "The back must be arched to keep from pitching forward, producing low-back pain. The shoulders are thrown back for the same reason; therefore we get shoulder pain. Since in most people one leg is slightly shorter than the other, the body tends to tilt to one side, making the neck pull to the other side, causing headaches. All this twisting results in wrinkles across the forehead," Dr. Kauth pointed out, before going on to add overlapping toes, aggravated bunions and hammer toes to the fruits of high-heeled and pointed-toe shoes.

Sling-back strip sandals would be OK if the heels were not high, he said. It is "wobbling all over the place in high-heeled sandals that causes puffy ankles and chronic ankle strain," Dr. Kauth believes. "Most of the disco dancers take their shoes off," he has noticed.

We have to take off those shoes to take back the freedom we had decided to forfeit in the shoe store. Incredibly, in 1978 women are (literally) following in the footsteps of the Chinese women, the Venetian women, the French women, the Turkish women, the Japanese women and millions of others too numerous to mention whose agony and constraints women are choosing in the shoe store of today.

For assistance in the research for this article we are indebted to Judy McGee and Gordon Stone of the Metropolitan Museum of Art Costume Institute and to Carol Morgan of the American Crafts Council.

EQUAL PAY

Separate and not equal in the workplace

Paula Kassell

This started out to be an article or two about why the earnings gap between women and men is continuing unchanged well into the second decade of the Equal Pay Act. We found that the problem has as many facets as a diamond and may be as hard to scratch. We now plan a continuing column.

Despite the fervent belief in "equal pay for equal work," few are aware that there is hardly any equal work.

Edward Kelly, the Women's Bureau economist who writes the annual earnings gap reports, says: "We can't compare wages in similar jobs because the average woman worker and the average man worker just don't have the same jobs." The earnings gap ratio has to be based on comparing the wages of all women and all men who work full time year round.

During the past 22 years, women earned, on the average, about 60 cents for every dollar earned by their male counterparts. In 1955 the ratio was at its highest — almost 64 cents. Since then it has dipped as low as 58 cents (1967). In 1977, the latest figure, it was under 59 cents: the median annual earnings of full-time, year-round women workers were only $8,618 while men's were $14,626. Professional women do a little better: $10,524 against $15,968.

One reason that no real change has occurred in the earnings gap, is that about 80 percent of the female workforce is in the low-paying, dead-end traditional female jobs and excluded from the lucrative traditional male jobs with potential. Women are:

¶ 91 percent of bank tellers, 25 percent of bank officials and managers,

¶ 88 percent of health service workers, 12 percent of physicians,

¶ 70 percent of school teachers, 29 percent of school administrators,

¶ 99 percent of secretaries, 18 percent of managers and administrators.

No change is expected in the foreseeable future.

Even in the occupations completely dominated by women, men are on the top of the salary heap. Among clerical workers (79 percent are women), women are earning 64 cents to the men's dollar. This is because in many companies there are several clerical grade levels or job titles. "The man off the street tends to be hired into one classification, the woman off the street into another," explained Frank McGowan, director of the Labor Department's Equal Pay Division.

Women who observe this can develop what he calls "a rational suspicion" that wage discrimination is taking place. And that is enough to warrant a complaint to the nearest equal pay enforce-

Linda Pryal, Executive Female Digest, publication of National Association for Female Executives

*Now I lay me down to sleep
I pray the Lord my job to keep
Should a woman take it someday
I thank the Lord she'll get less pay!*

ment office, listed in telephone directories under U.S. Government, Labor Department, Wage and Hour Division.

The division, not the suspicious woman, makes the investigation, and her name is held in strict confidence, as required by the Equal Pay Act. "Anonymity has worked absolutely," McGowan declared. "We don't even tell the employer we have a complaint." He is certain complainants' names will continue to be protected when the Equal Employment Opportunity Commission (EEOC) takes over Equal Pay Act enforcement from the Labor Department on July 1 of this year.

The enforcement agency can examine the company's pay scales and practices across the board, not just for the job or department that sparked the complaint. Ignoring job titles and grade classifications, the division looks for jobs with different pay scales although they are substantially equal in (1) responsibility, (2) education and training required, and (3) physical or mental effort needed. In this way, they come up with equal work within the definition of the law without having to find women and men doing exactly the same job.

It is easier to ferret out unequal pay for equal work hiding behind different job titles at low-skill levels. McGowan cited the "Girl Friday" who trains a parade of male administrative assistants who then pass her by on their way to the management ladder.

Notorious examples that have yielded to court suits and backpay settlements are female nurses' aides versus male orderlies, maids versus janitors, and inspectors versus packers. Other examples are retail buyers or salesclerks, where women handle "soft line" merchandise and are paid less than men handling "hard lines" such as major appliances.

Investigation of professional salaries uncovers inequities that are no different from those of maids and nurses' aides. A 1972 survey of chemists' salaries by the American Chemical Society showed that median salaries for men with bachelor degrees was $16,000 but for women was $12,500 (78¢ for women for each male dollar). For Ph.D.s the medians were $19,400 and $14,500 (75¢ on the dollar).

Examples could be cited endlessly, with every year's statistics for every profession yielding similar stories BECAUSE THE MEDIAN INCOME OF WOMEN COLLEGE GRADUATES IS LOWER THAN MEN'S WITH ONLY A HIGH-SCHOOL EDUCATION.

So each employed woman must either close her mind to the facts or speculate: Is my company (university, agency) an exception? Am I being paid as much as Mr. X? How can I know for sure?

© Copyright 1979 by Paula Kassell

The next column will describe the techniques women are developing to ferret out wage information where they work. If you have succeeded in finding out how your pay stacks up against the men's, let us know the methods you used. And what you did about it. If you have tried and failed, we want to know about that, too. Your identity will not be revealed if you so request.

EQUAL PAY ♀

Networks needed

Paula Kassell

"Find a network or found a network" is the answer on everyone's lips when the question is: "Am I getting equal pay?"

The network in this case is women interested in helping each other. It may be informal — a few women meeting for lunch to exchange information — or an organized women's association within a company — or any combination of the above.

It solves the problem of the individual woman looking at the few men around her, trying to determine whether her salary is equitable. There are too many variables — education, experience, skills, competence — and one can usually be cited to "explain" the men's higher pay, larger merit raises or earlier promotions.

Betty Harragan, who wrote Games Mother Never Taught You: Corporate Gamesmanship for Women (reviewed Autumn 1977), thinks the question is superfluous. "Start with the assumption that you are underpaid compared to equal male co-workers. All women are, and you are unlikely to be the sole exception . . . If you haven't asked for raises but merely accepted whatever was offered, your increases have been minimal compared to men . . . Inflation reduces everyone's salary . . . Just to stay even with last year's salary, you must get an increase to match current inflation losses. For example, if inflation is running at 5 percent, you need an annual increase of $500 on $10,000 or $750 on $15,000 before you can begin to calculate a meritorious raise."

Dr. Mary Rowe, Assistant to the Chancellor and President at Massachusetts Institute of Technology in Cambridge, suggests taking a look at the whole company and going right to top management for the information. The network, acting as a group and posing some serious questions, asks the company, in writing, to do a company-wide or departmental analysis and tell them the aggregate results:

• Are jobs classified correctly?
• Within each job classification are women and men with the same skills, experience and merit being paid the same?
• What constitutes similar jobs that should get similar pay?
• Have jobs been analyzed regarding the responsibility they entail?
• Are women and men being promoted and given merit raises at equivalent average age, education, merit and experience?

Just raising these questions raises the corporate consciousness: can top management afford not to know the answers? Rowe has found no corporation that has done such an analysis in the past 10 years that has not uncovered sex-discriminatory gaps.

> Woman has been the great unpaid laborer of the world . . . She is not paid according to the value of the work done, but according to sex.
> — Susan B. Anthony

One large corporation discovered in the early 1970s that at the time of promotion, women were older, better educated and more experienced as measured by the size of the budgets they controlled and the number of employees they supervised. So the company put in place a rigidly supervised posting system for all jobs. As a result of the huge number of over-qualified women in the lower ranks, during the first year 85 percent of the several hundred vertical moves within the company were made by women (both minority and non-minority). In six years, with 1,000 to 1,500 transfers a year taking place, the company wiped out the age-education-experience gap at the time of promotion.

Rowe makes the point that the success of a job-posting system depends on leaving practically no discretion in the hands of the departments. In this company all jobs were required to be posted for company-wide bidding, with only minor, clearly defined exceptions allowed:

• A qualified laid-off employee could be re-employed.
• If the department had no minority employees, a qualified outside minority candidate known to the department could be hired.
• A qualified candidate in the same office could be promoted.

It seems like a complex way to go about implementing the straightforward demand for equal pay. But years of frustration and helplessness have brought the realization that only through such complex arrangements backed up by committed management and watchful women will the tradition of paying women less be broken.

The right to equal pay — the feminist principle that everyone believes in, that seemed the most clearcut and easiest to monitor and implement — has proved to be the most illusive right of all.

For, in the Holy Bible (Leviticus 27), the worth of work was valued as follows: "And thy estimation shall be of the male from 20 years even unto 60 years, thy estimation shall be 50 shekels of silver . . . and if it be a female, then thy estimation shall be 30 shekels." By a strange and terrible coincidence, that 60 percent is the ratio between men's and women's wages in the 1970s.

© Copyright 1979 by Paula Kassell

If you have succeeded in finding out how your pay stacks up against the men's, let us know the methods you used. And what you did about it. If you have tried and failed, we want to know about that, too. Your identity will not be revealed if you so request.

EQUAL PAY ⚀
Any changes ahead?

Paula Kassell

The opening of the new decade has tempted many to prophesy the future of women in the labor market and in the family. The questions asked are: Will the present trends continue? What new trends might develop? Where will it all bring (or leave) women when this new decade ends?

The momentous changes that have already occurred as a result of the Women's Movement have left women pretty much where we were 15 years ago: (1) in women's jobs (2) with earnings less than 60 percent of men's and (3) still responsible for the housework and child-rearing. Today there are just millions more of us described by all of the above.

What are the connections between what is happening in the home and workplace?

The statistics showing that only a small proportion of families are traditional is misleading, according to Alice Rossi, a professor of sociology who was a founder of the National Organization for Women. The statistics: only 16 percent of households in the United States consist of the father as the only wage earner, a mother as a full-time homemaker and at least one child at home. More than half of all mothers with children under age 18 are in the labor force. Even the presence of a child under 6 years of age is not the barrier it used to be — 41 percent of their mothers are employed.

But going out to work does not improve the status of women — the work we do on the job is in the tradition of helping others and deriving satisfaction from that (as in homemaking), Rossi reminds us. Equal pay checks in the family are required for equality inside the family — otherwise his time is worth more than hers.

Time studies and opinion polls bear Rossi out. NOW tried but did not succeed in presenting four egalitarian couples at its National Assembly on the Future of the Family last November. Even the most determinedly feminist couples find it impossible to structure a non-sexist family environment for their children.

So it is not surprising that in the average family, working mothers spend only slightly fewer hours at home-making than do professional housewives. Alice Cook, a professor of industrial relations who has studied the family in many countries, concludes that husbands do not "really put their backs to it when their wives go to work . . . either in the communist countries or in Sweden or elsewhere . . . As the multinational time budget research in twelve countries amply demonstrates, the husband spends very little more time assisting the wife and other with household tasks when she works outside the home . . . Studies make clear that husbands and children, when they help at all, tend to assist only with selected, often self-selected, tasks . . ."

As our daughters observe their mothers, juggling their double burdens, no wonder they are consciously or subconsciously saying "no thanks" and opting for the traditional dependency of their grandmothers. That does not leave much hope that future families will be more egalitarian as the generations pass.

Nor does this generation of American husbands intend to change. A recent research report on "What Today's Man Wants From Today's Woman," by BBDO, an advertising agency, came up with:

• Above all else, he believes a woman should be a good mother.

• But, in addition, today's man wants a woman to be intelligent, ambitious and self-confident.

• He approves of her going out to work but wants her to be sure to take care of the household chores, and the shopping, and the kids.

While 82 percent of men say they approve of working mothers, 59 percent of men would rather not work with a woman.

This 1979 study, based on males between the ages of 18-50 in 20 American cities, reiterates the findings of a 1969 study of males in their senior year on a liberal college campus. Ninety-three percent of them "qualified their acceptance of a wife's career with the expectation that it not interfere with their own careers or the efficient operation of their homes. Only 7 percent of these young men (who would now be in their early or mid-thirties) expressed willingness to significantly modify their own career and domestic roles in order to "facilitate their future wives' careers."

"If American men and women are only comfortable in marriages based on an invidious relationship between husband and wife, can they be expected to accept a different, even reversed, relationship in public life?" asked Judith Stiehm, a professor of political science, on the op-ed page of The New York Times. "If those who are best-educated, and with the highest status and highest income — in short, the decision-making men in our society — dominate, outstrip, and are deferred to by their wives, can they be expected to perceive other women as peers? Can women achieve high levels of public excellence while maintaining a carefully arranged marital deference?"

Now the vicious circle is exposed: Inequality at home leads to inequality on the job leads to inequality at home . . .

Each one of us has the power and the opportunity to shatter that chain reaction, whether we start at home or at the workplace, and whether we attack it alone or joined with others.

©1979 by Paula Kassell

For some provocative forecasting about the workplace and families: THE SUBTLE REVOLUTION: Women at Work, edited by Ralph E. Smith (Publications Office, The Urban Institute, 2100 M St., NW, Washington, DC 20037) hardcover, No. URI 26800, $15., paperback, No. 26700, $7.50.

EQUAL PAY
♀
Women are winning

Paula Kassell

Women are winning their job discrimination cases. Though the process can seem endless, the payoffs for the women who start the actions and for thousands of other women are huge. So it is worth while to take a look at the trophies.

The grandmommy of all is the 1973 AT&T case, the first big consent decree obtained by the federal Equal Employment Opportunity Commission (EEOC). AT&T agreed to pay $38 million in restitution and back pay to women and minorities. But that is history.

Savor these:

• General Electric agreed to a $32 million settlement in 1978. Charges were brought by the EEOC in 1973.

• Chase Manhattan Bank reached a settlement with the federal Office of Contract Compliance costing $2 million in 1978, after a group of women sued the bank in 1976. It was the US Labor Department's first employment conciliation agreement with a major bank.

• Uniroyal agreed to $5.2 million in back pay to women employees after the Labor Department barred the company, the nation's third largest tire manufacturer, from receiving federal contracts because of sex discrimination. The case had dragged on for seven years. Women employees had filed a private suit against the company in 1972. Then, in 1975, they brought suit against the labor department, itself, asking it to move against the company.

• Hoffmann-LaRoche, the pharmaceutical giant that developed and grew rich on Valium, agreed in 1979 to more than $1 million in back pay for about 400 women employees, after a 1978 review of its employment practices by the Labor Department. A $9 million contract with the Defense Department was at stake.

• The City of Chicago was ordered in 1978 to pay $2.98 million in damages to women. The class action suit was filed by the National Organization for Women in 1974. Individual awards ranged from $1,000 to $52,880.

• Bechtel, the nation's largest construction company, settled for $1.4 million in back wages to female employees in 1979. The company signed a consent decree with the EEOC after two months of trial.

• Liberty Mutual Life Insurance Company established a $4 million fund in 1979, to be divided among past and current women employees according to length of service. The settlement was said to be the largest ever secured by private litigants for sex discrimination in employment under the Civil Rights Act. The suit was filed in 1972.

• The Consolidation Coal Company of Pittsburgh signed a voluntary agreement in 1978 to give $370,000 to 78 women who were denied jobs at its mines. The cash payments were negotiated by the Department of Interior. No litigation was involved—the company admitted the problem and expressed a willingness to make amends, a department attorney said.

• Merck and Company, a major pharmaceutical manufacturer, signed a $3.2 million agreeemnt with the Labor Department in 1979 after compliance reviews and complaint investigations. An employee group known as Women of Merck had filed the complaint in 1975.

"…agreed to"…"agreed to",,,"agreed to"…over and over. Of course they agreed to settle. The cases were sound (discrimination is all too obvious in most companies). Dragging through court action might have cost them more in back pay and attorneys' fees for both sides—and certainly cost them more in damaged reputation as proof of their discrimination was aired in public.

That's why women are winning. And this is worth thinking about: because the enforcement agencies are investigating employment patterns and practices and instituting class action suits, one or two women can blow the whistle on a corporate giant or an entire industry.

Brilliant — but beautiful and blonde

Mary Cunningham was thoroughly equipped by education (Phi Beta Kappa, Wellesley; MBA, Harvard Business School) and experience (financial analyst, Chase Manhattan Bank; mergers and acquisitions, Salomon Brothers, investment bankers) for promotion to vice president for strategic planning of the Bendix Corporation. That appointment followed her brilliant performance as executive assistant to William Agee, head of the corporation, and then as vice president for corporate and public affairs. "If there's a woman in America who can become chief executive officer of a Fortune 500 company any time in the next 10 years—on ability—it's Mary," James Heskett told the women students association when he was chair of the Harvard Business School MBA department. No woman could have been less in need of performing sexually to advance her career.

But Mary Cunningham was also young (29), slender (size 6), and beautiful, with long strawberry blonde hair.

So the rumors started. Agee met them head on by telling a meeting of Bendix employees that they were "close friends." With that dry bone to lick, the newspapers and wire services began to inflate a rumor without a scintilla of evidence into a sex scandal. To the mass media, such a woman's body is so newsworthy that it overshadows such a woman's mind. To the sexist—and what is the media if not sexist—it must be the body that accounts for the attainments. The rumor and resignation whipped the press into a frenzy. The New York Times ran eleven pieces in 24 days—news reports, a correction, analyses, columns, interviews and an editorial. The New York Daily News ran a five-part biography of Mary Cunningham by Gail Sheehy, based on interviews started over a year ago. The Washington Post and the Washington Star ran it, too, and the Post is sore because it thought it had an exclusive. These east-coast antics are reflected in the cross-country coverage of this story. Bendix, after all, is head-quartered in Michigan, with 80,000 employees in many locations in the United States and around the world. The more publicity Cunningham's story gets, the more questions remain:

- First and foremost, would there have been a resignation if there had been no press frenzy?
- As a result of this incident, will men be more hesitant—indeed afraid—to promote women?
- Will plain women now get ahead faster than pretty women?
- Is the "feminine woman" now at a disadvantage?
- Is "acting more like a man" any more acceptable now than it ever was?
- Did William Agee use bad judgment in discussing the matter at an employees' meeting?
- Will Agee have to resign?
- If Mary Cunningham had been William Agee's boss, which one would have resigned?
- And, finally, what is to become of Mary Cunningham?

Paula Kassell

EQUAL PAY

Media still in control of white males

Paula Kassell

The New York Times story on the opening of the international women's conference in Copenhagen last July was printed on the "style" page right next to a recipe for sardine salad sandwiches.

Obviously the men who manage The Times believe a United Nations conference of over 1,000 official delegates from 145 countries is not "news." There is a connection between the way women's activities are covered by the media and the low positions of women in the media (of course, we speak here of the non-feminist media).

Women journalists who file discrimination suits have recognized this, and one of their aims in pressing to move women up into positions of control is to improve the final product that now reaches the public from the hands and minds of an almost totally white male hierarchy:

DAILY & SUNDAY NEWSPAPERS

Job	Women	Men	Percent Male
Editor in Chief	0	20	100
Senior Editor	0	9	100
Editor	64	1,111	95
Assoc. Editor	23	140	86
Ass't. Editor	6	16	73
Executive Editor	6	232	97
Ass't Exec. Editor	1	6	86
Managing Editor	75	962	93
Assoc. Managing Ed.	1	11	92
Ass't. Managing Ed.	28	217	89
Deputy Managing Ed.	0	9	100
Editorial Chief	28	317	92
	232	3,050	93

BROADCASTING

	TV		Radio	
Job	Women	Men	Women	Men
News Director	5	95	11	89
News Staff	26	74	26	74

FILM DIRECTORS

	Directed By		Percent
	Women	Men	Male
Network Prime Time Dramatic TV Hours	115	65,385	98
Feature Films By Major Distributors	14	7,332	99
Directing Assignments Theatrical Features	1	77	99
TV Movies	1	116	99
TV Episodes	23	1,571	99
Pilots & Mini-series	1	138	99

Eventually we may see some changes as the discrimination suits that women have won begin to take effect. Virtually all of them have been settled out of court (the newspapers and broadcasters do not want their dirty linen aired in the public eye), and virtually all of them require affirmative action to hire and advance women:

● **NBC** settled out of court, promising to bring more women into management and technical positions, $540,000 for lump sum back pay and a $3 million fund for merit pay (1977).

● **Reader's Digest** settled out of court, promising to carry out an elaborate scheme to place women in many job categories, $200,000 in "pay adjustments" and $1,375,000 in "settlement payments" (1978).

● **KOIN-TV** (Oregon)—after the Portland chapter of the National Organization for Women (NOW) petitioned the FCC to take away its broadcast license, the channel agreed to set up a women's advisory council on programming and employment, increase top jobs for women and minorities, equalize fringe benefits and even sponsor equal sports teams. (1978).

● **The New York Times** settled out of court, promising a four-year affirmative action plan that included every level of management, even unto the top corporate officers, $233,500 in back pay and up to $100,000 in attorneys' fees and expenses (1978). For a fascinating true story stranger than fiction, read the Times internal man-to-man memos on personnel matters and the court testimony of Times officials included in Women and The New York Times published by Media Report to Women (address below).

● **KOA Stations** (Denver) settled out of court with a $60,000 payment to two women. A case worth reporting, though small. One woman was denied a promotion because she was considered a feminist, and the other was told she was "audacious" to consider herself (a female) a potential manager. Both were fired. Their complaint charged retaliation (1979).

● **Associated Press**—EEOC filed suit asserting that AP "fails to recruit and hire females for news positions on the same basis as it recruits and hires male newspersons." AP had refused to accept the goals and timetables in the affirmative action plan proposed by EEOC (1979; not settled yet).

● **Detroit News**—class action suit filed on behalf of all Detroit News women, charging that men received higher salaries than women for substantially the same work and that women are intentionally denied challenging, growth assignments (1979; not settled yet).

● **Washington Post** settled out of court, promising a five-year "good faith effort" to fill at least one-third of the officials, managers and professional jobs in news and editorial that become available, with similar goals in the commercial and advertising departments—plus $104,000 in monetary awards, $42,500 in legal fees and $100,000 for new scholarships and sabbatical leaves (1981).

I was planning to write a concluding paragraph but women can draw our own conclusions as we monitor what is selected for presentation as news in the non-feminist media and note that our important meetings and achievements are not covered. For the general public, if it's not in the news, it didn't happen.

Sources: Newspaper management staffs—Dorothy Jurney; broadcast management staffs—Vernon A. Stone; film directors—Directors' Guild of America Women's Committee. Those data and news about discrimination suits excerpted from Media Report to Women—monthly, $15-year (personal check), $20 (institutions). Information located through Media Report to Women Index Directory—annual, $8. Women and The New York Times ($2.50). All from Women's Institute for Freedom of the Press, 3306 Ross Place, NW, Washington, DC 20008; telephone (202) 363-0812.

©1981 Paula Kassell

By any other name

When people say they oppose affirmative action to redress discrimination because they want to "return" to the merit system, don't you believe it. We never had a merit system. We have always had affirmative action—for a friend, for a member of the right club, for the football star, and for the son-in-law (for example, the two men who married the owner's daughter and became publishers—of The New York Times and the Washington Post).

Ronald Reagan opposes affirmative action to redress discrimination while using affirmative action to appoint his campaign aides to high positions for which they have little or no background. Nothing new about that. His is certainly not the first political regime to reward backers with jobs. Perhaps it is even expected and accepted.

What galls is crying out of one side of the mouth that affirmative action will force the hiring of incompetent people, while naming political cronies to big jobs out of the other.

Reagan can take affirmative action away from us, but the Civil Rights Act is not likely to be repealed even by the present Congress. The only solution is to bid for the jobs we qualify for, hold employers to the letter of the laws against discrimination, and keep pushing hard on the compliance agencies and the courts to enforce them.

NEW DIRECTIONS FOR WOMEN can ferret out the facts and keep our readers up-to-date and aware. Women have to take it from there.

Paula Kassell

EQUAL PAY

Paula Kassell

Betty Friedan has been saying we have to move into the second stage of the women's movement, no longer against men, but with them.

She has it backwards: it's men who have to be moved into a new stage.

The locus of our problems has always been the (male-female) family, is still the family and will be the family until we change the division of responsibilities, and thus the relationship, between women and men.

Commentators have been telling us that truth over and over again for many decades. We have not acted on it except in discouragingly superficial ways. So the heterosexual family has changed only infinitesimally in the decade and a half since the current women's movement began, while a whole new generation has married, set up sexist households and proceeded to raise children in almost the same old sexist ways.

I want to share with you the fruits of my research:

No nation can be free when half the population is enslaved in the kitchen.

Lenin

Women are still the primary child-rearer, even when they work, and the purpose of their work, in the main, is to support and advance the family, not to realize themselves as individuals.

Carl N. Degler, At Odds

Men may cook, or weave, or dress dolls, or hunt hummingbirds, but if such activities are appropriate occupations of men, then the whole society, men and women alike, votes them as important. When the same occupations are performed by women, they are regarded as less important.

Margaret Mead, Male and Female

Why would anyone want to research housework? The very word evokes centuries of drudgery. This drudgery, Dr. Ann Oakley realized, has been ignored by history, economics, and sociology, and thus woman's work has been dispensed with historically forever.

Vera Goodman, "English author exposes housework's dirty deal," interview with Ann Oakley, New Directions for Women, Spring 1977.

Axioms supporting the invisibility of women's work:
(1) Women belong in the family, while men belong "at work";
(2) therefore men work, while women do not work;
(3) therefore housework is not a form of work.

Ann Oakley, The Sociology of Housework

More axioms:
(4) monetary and social rights belong to those who work—to those who are economically productive;
(5) women do not work but are parasitic;
(6) therefore women are not entitled to the same social and economic rights as men.
THUS THE INVISIBILITY OF THEIR WORK PROVIDES A RATIONAL FOR WOMEN'S SECOND—CLASS STATUS IN BOTH PUBLIC AND PRIVATE DOMAINS.

Nona Glazer—Malbin, "Housework," Signs, Summer 1976

Single, married or divorced, regardless of whether she holds a paid job or not, a woman is a housewife, at least part of her life. Even if she can afford to hire another woman to do her housework, the responsibility for running the household is hers....As long as unpaid housework is by definition woman's work, all the work of women will be downgraded. The gender linking of service functions is at the root of woman's problem in society. The fact that every woman is a housewife, and that every housewife is a woman structures inequality between the sexes into every institution of society...The problem of the

housewife, for so long considered minor and insignificant, something to be solved within the family and the household, is actually social and political, much more than personal. It is a problem which can only be solved by a restructuring of all institutions of society and by creating new forms of community.
                                    Gerda Lerner, "The American
                                    Housewife: A Historical Perspective,
                                    **Feminist Perspectives on Housework
                                    and Child Care**

Her resume listing decades of budgeting, mediating, managing, creating, decision—making, nurturing, and physical and mental exertion in the home, school and community, elicits from the job interviewer a sentence that chills the soul, "Aha, I see you haven't worked in twenty years."

A few years back, Funk and Wagnalls Dictionary defined a housewife as "one who doesn't work for a living." Yet during the same period, a Chase Manhattan Bank study found that homemakers work up to 99 hours a week at 12 different tasks....

One woman reports that for a few days her husband did all the cleaning, washing, shopping, cooking and child care because he'd read that if a housewife isn't too tired, she's a better sex partner. Did it work? "I never found out," she says. "He was too tired."
                                    Letty Cottin Pogrebin, "Rethinking
                                    Housework," **Feminist Perspectives on Housework**

Husband: "Housework is too trivial to even talk about." Meaning: It's even more trivial to do. Housework is beneath my status. My purpose is life is to deal with matters of significance. Yours is to deal with matters of insignificance. You should do the housework.
                                    Pat Mainardi, "The Politics of Housework,"
                                    Sisterhood is Powerful

Some day, perhaps, a conference on housework and child care will have as many male participants as female and they will be speaking from their own experience on the subject. Wouldn't that be nice!
                                    Marjorie Lipsyte, "Conference hits housewife
                                    woes," **New Directions for Women,** Winter 1977-78

You must ooze love from every pore, for your work, your husband and your children. This might require a 31-hour day, and if you wonder when you'll get time to rest, well, you can sleep in your old age if you live that long. You may be disappointed if you fail, but you are doomed if you don't try.
                                    Beverly Sills, addressing the 557 women graduates.
                                    Barnard College graduation, 1981

"I used to take pride in being a Superwoman," said a Manhattan woman listening to Friedan (at a symposium on the future of the family). "Now I see it, not as a personal victory but as a failure. A failure of my relationship with my husband, a failure of the work world, maybe even a failure of the society that just isn't adjusting to the way we live."
                                    Ellen Goodman, "Saying No the
                                    Superwoman," **The Boston Globe**

I feel, as never before, that this whole question of women's rights turns on the pivot of the marriage relations, and mark my word, sooner or later, it will be the topic for discussion.
                                    Elizabeth Cady Stanton, letter
                                    to Susan B. Anthony, 1853

For the funniest, sharpest insights send for **The Politics of Housework** by Pat Mainardi, written way back in 1968. Publication No. 078 from KNOW, INC., P.O. Box 86031, Pittsburgh, PA 15221. $1.00

© Copyright 1981 Paula Kassell

EQUAL PAY

Nurses assume new militancy over pay

Paula Kassell

The nurse is the ultimate female worker—nurturing, dedicated, loyal—proficient and underpaid.

Across the country, the average staff nurse earns $14,000 a year, according to the American Nurses' Association (ANA). That salary looks good to a recent graduate, but five years later she may be earning $16,000. There's not much reward for longevity and no real room for mobility if she prefers hands-on patient care to administrative work. Like the housewife-mother, the nurse is expected to feel compensated by the importance of the humble tasks she performs in making patients comfortable and speeding their recovery.

But that is no longer enough. The humble tasks no longer satisfy. Nurses say they are torn about doing it, but they are leaving the profession because they are not allowed to provide the care and exercise the judgment they were trained to do, while a large part of their day is spent on housekeeping chores. When the ANA negotiates contracts as a labor union, autonomy and a voice on the hospital's policy-making board are on the agenda along with salary and working hours.

Atlanta district members went so far as to picket an American College of Surgeons meeting to confront the doctors over the way they treat nurses. They called it "informational picketing" because they handed the doctors brochures that read: "Dear Doctor: Are you aware of doing or have you seen your colleagues do any of the following?

• "Treat a nurse as your secretary? Or as your assistant when you could easily have done something yourself and you knew it wasn't her task?

• "Did you abuse or insult her in front of a patient when you were in fact at fault?

• "Did you fail to learn the names of any of the nurses on staff because you felt their contribution was so negligible as not to deserve any recognition?"

The nurses were surprised at the reaction of the surgeons. Many of them said, "Yes, either I have or my colleagues have. We didn't know it was bothering you. We'll try to work on it."

The big question is: If nurses are treated better, will they trade off higher salaries for job satisfaction? That's what women are expected to do.

Right now the answer seems to be, "No!" Though nursing service is still only a small component of the total hospital bill, nurses' salaries have risen at higher rates than the Consumer Price Index, doctors' fees and other hospital medical services. But they are not yet in line with the competing jobs in industry that have been siphoning nurses out of their profession.

Only about 70 percent of the country's RNs are active, while the American Hospital Association reports a national shortage of 100,000. So hospitals must compete with each other.

The New Directions for Women office is directly across the street from Pascack Valley Hospital, Westwood, NJ We have twice had the painful experience of watching striking nurses picketing. During a 40-day strike in 1977 and a 70-day strike in 1979 we watched them march in rain and brutal cold. Now a new hospital administrator who took over in April of this year has voluntarily renegotiated the 1979 contract to increase the wage provisions. Pascack Valley's nurses are now getting wages that are higher than at any other area hospital.

For a change we are actually seeing market competition forcing up female wage rates, overcoming the pernicious prevailing wage.

But the positive story of Pascack Valley is not taking place in many towns. In general turnover rates are about 25 percent a year. In some hospitals only the sickest patients get nursing care. Intensive care nurses must sometimes work double shifts! Temporary nurses who might not know the hospital's routines are becoming common.

All of this is at the expense of the patient's well-being. Overworked nurses cannot be expected to answer the call bell promptly or to be sweet-tempered when they do. (The problem is so pervasive that a strategy book has hit the market, **The Patient's Advocate: The Complete Handbook of Patient's Rights** by Barbara Huttman (Penguin) $8.95.)

The marketplace already knows that it takes lots of money to buy engineers, advertising copywriters, corporate managers and even doctors. It seems it is only very slowly learning that it also takes money to buy Tender Loving Care.

© 1981 Paula Kassell

VISITING NURSE makes her rounds in the late 19th century.
To Be A Woman in America 1850-1930 by Annette K. Baxter (Times Book $7.95)

Turning the tables on Mormon missionaries

Paula Kassell

One morning the doorbell rang just as I was pulling an old ERA T-shirt over my head. At the door were two clean-cut young men neatly dressed in dark business suits, white shirts and black ties.

"We're from the Mormon Church," one said. Obviously they were Mormon missionaries. I knew that many young Mormon men spent a year or two as missionaries, going from door-to-door trying to convert strangers.

"We'd better not waste each other's time," I told them. "Look what I'm wearing." I swung open the door so they could see the letters E.R.A. written across my ample bosom.

MM: "The church believes in equal rights for women. We just don't believe that the ERA will be good for women."

PK: "But without a constitutional amendment, the rights women have been given by law can be taken away by Congress or state legislatures at any time. Equal pay for equal work, for instance, could be repealed. So could our credit rights. And there are still state laws that discriminate against one sex or the other. It would take hundreds of years to change them one by one. Thousands of court cases would be generated, and without the clear constitutional requirement not to discriminate by sex, courts in different states would make opposite rulings. They are doing that right now. Equal rights for women must be spelled out in the Constitution once and for all."

issue of New Directions For Women next to the door, ready to take to a meeting. On the front cover is a picture of Sonia Johnson at an ERA rally. She is the devout Mormon woman who was excommunicated from the church because she spoke out in favor of the ERA in spite of the official church position against it. I held the picture up in front of them.

PK: "Do you know who that is?"

MM: "Yes."

PK: "This issue also has a four-page ERA SPECIAL centerfold of information about the Equal Rights Amendment."

I showed him the text of the amendment on the first page of the ERA section and read it out loud.

MM: "Is that the whole amendment?"

PK: "Yes. You can see that the amendment has nothing to do with abortion or integrating public toilets or all the other things that have been used to frighten people. Look at this list of 16 states that already have state equal rights amendments or clauses in their constitutions, some of them for many years. Not one state has integrated public toilets or forced women to go to work to share in the support of her children. That's still purely a family decision in every state that already has an equal rights provision in its own constitution."

MM: "If the ERA passes, won't women have to be drafted?"

PK: "Yes. Let me tell you that it bothers me just as much to have my son drafted as to think of my daughter being drafted. My son is just as precious to me as my daughter. Under the ERA, women would have to be treated equally with men and be required to register for the draft if men were. You know there are tens of thousands of women in all branches of the armed forces now, on a voluntary basis. I personally don't understand why any woman would want to be in the Army, but I believe that those who do want to serve should have the freedom of choice. I don't think it's fair to deprive women of the training and educational opportunities and pensions provided by military service. As for combat duty, you know only a very small percentage of the men in the armed forces ever see combat duty. Not all men are suited for it and probably some women are.

The young men listened to all this with rapt attention, though one was silent throughout and the other asked all the questions. To that one I said:

PK: "If I give you this copy of NEW DIRECTIONS FOR WOMEN, will you promise to read it, especially the four pages about the Equal Rights Amendment?"

MM: "Yes, I promise. I do like to keep informed."

He folded the paper carefully and put it in his jacket pocket. We had spent five or ten minutes together, and as they went down the walk, I thought, "Today I was a missionary to the Mormons, and on my own front porch." But I was sorry I hadn't given them Sonia Johnson's address: Mormons for ERA, Rt. 2, Box 233, Sterling, VA 22170. Because their open-minded interest surprised me.

Speaking personally

Mormon Missionary: "We're here to talk about the church, not the ERA."

Paula Kassell: "I know quite a bit about the Mormon Church and its history. I've known several Mormons personally and have found them to be exceptionally fine people. But I don't agree with the teachings of the Mormon Church."

MM: "But we believe a man should be the head of the family."

PK: "Well, the Equal Rights Amendment has nothing to do with that. All it has to do with are the laws that can be passed by Congress and the states. It has nothing to say about families or who must go to work, or anything like that. Do you know what it actually says?"

MM: "No, I've never seen it. Do you have a copy I could look at?"

I just happened to have a stack of the September-October 1981

Ruth Abnholz

EQUAL PAY

Open the workplace to women's charities

Paula Kassell

Fund-raising at the workplace is the best and cheapest way to solicit money for non-profit health, welfare, service and advocacy organizations.

The United Way raised $1.53 billion in 1980. The Combined Federal Campaign, which solicits federal government employees, raised $90 million.

Women are now over 46 percent of the total labor force. The question is: Are we getting an equal opportunity to donate our money where we want to? Given a chance to choose, women might be expected to designate a local child care center or battered women's shelter, or a national organization that provides legal services in sex discrimination cases.

WHEN DONORS ARE GIVEN WIDER CHOICE IN DESIGNATING WHERE THEY WANT THEIR MONEY TO GO, RESULTS INDICATE THAT GIVING INCREASES. The newsletter of the National Committee for Responsive Philanthropy reported: "In Philadelphia, a huge controversy caused United Way to allow employees to make on-the-job gifts to non-United Way charities. More than a thousand charities benefitted from this...

"The charity that was at the heart of the controversy—Women's Way—raised more than $100,000 in workplace gifts, the highest total for any non-United Way charity. In addition, the six charities which are members of Women's Way got $18,000 in gifts specifically designated for them.

"The overall effect of opening up the United Way drive is one more testament to the value of open workplace charity drives. Total giving went up more than 16 percent in Philadelphia compared to a 7.4 percent average increase for United Way nationally."

Non-profit women's services, along with minority groups, have been fighting to be included in the United Way and federal campaigns for years, but they are being effectively stonewalled. A few chinks have been chipped away, as in Philadelphia. In 1981 the NOW Legal Defense and Education Fund and the Federally Employed Women's FEW Legal and Education Fund were accepted by the Combined Federal Campaign—they are the only women's organizations ever admitted. Being accepted meant only that they had the privilege of applying individually to about 550 federal sites, each of which has its own criteria and committee which must be convinced that the organization does something to benefit, directly or indirectly, the local population. And every year every organization must reapply on both the federal and local level, said Kent Bailey of the Office of Personnel Management, which administers the federal drive.

In 1981 the NOW fund was given three weeks between the time it was notified of its eligibility and the date the applications were due at the 550 local sites, said Ann Simon, the fund's counsel. It decided to apply to the top 100 sites, which contribute 80 percent of the total raised. It was accepted by about 30, rejected by 35 and did not hear from the rest.

The FEW fund managed to apply to about 500 sites. They were accepted by 150, rejected by about the same number, and never heard from the rest, said Terry Hart Lee, president.

The funds will not learn the amounts they will receive until about March.

In 1980 the Women's Legal Defense Fund got $60,000 in the Washington, DC federal campaign, and Equal Rights Advocates got $3,000 in the San Francisco Bay Area federal campaign because of another chink chipped in the stone wall: local organizations not in the United Way were declared eligible to apply to local federal campaigns.

But even these small changes are in jeopardy, according to Robert Bothwell, executive director of the National Committee for Responsive Philanthropy. The Office of Personnel Management, which makes the rules for the Combined Federal Campaign, is considering narrower eligibility criteria, allowing only charities providing a narrow range of health and welfare services to solicit federal employees. This would exclude community development and neighborhood organizing groups as well as organizations, such as the women's funds, engaged in public education, research and litigation. This blow is being considered at the very time that President Reagan is shifting heavy responsibilities to private giving.

The suggested restrictions take on an ominous tinge cast by the large shadow of United Way. It was United Way that submitted the proposal to narrow eligibility, said Bothwell.

We can see the handwriting on United Way's own stone wall. Even now United Way campaigns remain virtually closed to women's concerns.

What can women employees do about that? Everything! We are in complete control. In addition to making direct contributions to feminist organizations, we can refuse to contribute to fund drives that do not serve the needs we consider important. We can urge, insist and ultimately force United Way and all workplace fund drives to open the coffers to minority and women's organizations.

Now is the time to pressure for change, while they are counting the 1981 take, analyzing last fall's campaign, and making plans for 1982 and beyond. Here are the addresses you need:

United Way of America, 801 North Fairfax St., Alexandria, VA 22314; (703) 836-7100.

Combined Federal Campaign, United States Office of Personnel Management, Washington, DC 20415; (202) 655-4000. President Ronald Reagan, The White House, Washington, DC; (202) 456-1414.

National Committee for Responsive Philanthropy, 810 18 St., NW, Washington, DC 20006; (202) 347-5340. The committee was formed to increase the accountability and accessibility of philanthropic institutions—fund drives, foundations, corporations. Annual dues: $15, includes quarterly newsletter.

Copyright 1982 Paula Kassell

Bad swap!

There just has to be a hidden agenda behind President Reagan's proposal to take administration of the Medicaid program away from the states and transfer it all to Washington. The logical suspicion is that he wants complete control of abortion funding. Further disaster for poor women would be the inevitable result.

Since a June 1980 ruling from the all-male Supreme Court, the federal government has been under no obligation to fund abortions for poor women, with only one exception—"her life would be endangered if the fetus came to term." However, nine states, Alaska, Colorado, Hawaii, Maryland, Michigan, New York, North Carolina, Oregon and Washington, and the District of Columbia have been paying for abortions with state funds. Five additional states have continued to pay for abortions under state court orders: California, Connecticut, Massachusetts, New Jersey and Pennsylvania.

Statistics indicate that in the 14 states that still finance Medicaid abortions, almost 98 percent of the women who sought an abortion did obtain one. Because these states include several that are densely populated and about 75 percent of all the women eligible for Medicaid live in them, the federal ban has so far had much less effect than expected.

Still, the National Center for Disease Control reported that, since the Hyde amendment severely restricting federal abortion funding went into effect in 1977, about 5 percent of the women who might have sought abortions continued their pregnancies to term, resulting in an estimated 14,000 births. Looking back to the fiscal year just before the Hyde amendment took effect, about 295,000 abortions were paid for by a combination of state and federal Medicaid funds.

Contrast that with this figure: the federal government has been paying for about 3,000 abortions a year under the Supreme Court license to deny.

Once control is transferred to the federal government, the states are out of the Medicaid business. And what state is likely to fund abortions from its depleted budget? The National Governors Association is already contending that swapping Medicaid for welfare with Washington would cost the states at least $9 million.

The inevitable prospect is that poor women in all 50 states and the District of Columbia will lose government-funded abortions unless their very lives depend on it. Rape or incest is no excuse.

Some safety net.

Paula Kassell

Male pride equals too many children

Paula Kassell

As Perdita Huston talked to poor village women in six different countries, she heard the same dreams of the future: not as many children as their mothers had—a few children and to be able to feed them better, dress them properly, and send them to school.

So why are these women in Tunisia, Egypt, Sudan, Kenya, Sri Lanka and Mexico having so many children? One woman gave the answer that could have been given in all six countries: "My husband says, 'The village will laugh at me if my wife doesn't have a child every year'." MANHOOD EQUALS FERTILITY (not responsibility). Huston pointed out. Out of 207 women to whom she spoke, only two (Mexican) said they were using contraceptives without their husband's knowledge. Universally, the situation was that this was a subject they could not even discuss with their husbands. The typical statement was: "If I don't give him a child every year, he will go and get another wife. Then what will the children and I do?"

Behind the women's assent and acceptance of the men's macho behavior is fear and utter dependence. Under the legal status of women in the Third World, women must please their husbands: "Husbands can divorce them at will, take another wife at will, and beat them at will, Huston told the UN Decade for Women Committee after her return. Even when the laws of the country have been modified to protect women from these abuses, often the rural women are not even aware of that.

Huston is a former Peace Corps Regional Director of North Africa, the Near East, Asia and the Pacific, and was a member of the US delegation to the 1980 UN women's conference in Copenhagen. She traveled in the six countries under a grant from the UN Fund for Population Activities.

She talked with women in the fields, markets, clinics and offices, and in their homes, in small group sessions, sometimes followed by one-to-one interviews with those willing to reveal their lives, problems and innermost dreams. She took no photographs and guaranteed anonymity. The questions she asked them were: What are your hopes for the future? What do you most want to learn? How is your life different from your mother's or grandmother's?

For the illiterate village women, the dream is of survival—learning how to grow more food to feed their families and how to keep their children healthy. They want to learn how to market their craft work and how to keep accounts. The changing economy in the developing countries has created a need for cash, and the middleman now gets the bulk of the cash for the women's craft work.

For the next higher level of women—those who already have some education—the dream is to be able to teach the other women. They want to learn management skills and how to talk in public. They want to develop competence and the confidence to go to government and agency officials to ask for help for their programs.

Women have gained enough confidence to start schools, water distribution projects and farm cooperatives. Huston visited cooperative child care centers, stores, and housing projects started by women's groups with the help of small loans (but credit is still a pervasive problem for women not accompanied by a man).

So there are glimmers of hope that women in these countries will slowly gain control of their lives, but that is still in the future.

The book describing the interviews is well worth reading for a detailed view of women's lives and thoughts:

THIRD WORLD WOMEN SPEAK OUT: Interviews in Six Countries on Change, Development, and Basic Needs by Perdita Huston (Praeger) $4.95 from Overseas Development Council, 1717 Massachusetts Ave., NW, Washington, DC 20036.

Further reading:

WOMEN AND WORLD DEVELOPMENT with annotated bibliography edited by Irene Tinker, Michele Bo Bramsen and Mayra Buvinic (Overseas Development Council, address above) $6.95.

BRINGING WOMEN INTO THE COMMUNITY DEVELOPMENT PROCESS: A PRAGMATIC APPROACH by Marion Fennelly Levy (Save the Children) $2.50 from Save the Children, 54 Wilton Road, Westport, CT 06880.

FAMILY PHOTOGRAPHS

1. My parents, Bertha and Daniel Kassell (Atlantic City, NJ, 1920s)

2. A Junior (Barnard College, 1938)

3. With my husband, Gerson Friedman (honeymoon, Atlantic City, NJ, 1941)

4. My sister Beatrice with Harris Friedman, her fiance - my husband Gerson's brother (Lake Hopatcong, NJ, 1940)

5. With Gerson's and my children, Daniel and Claire, in our front yard
(Dover, NJ, 1946)

6. With Gerson, reading to our grandchildren, Michael and Julia Foodman
(Reading, MA, 1980)

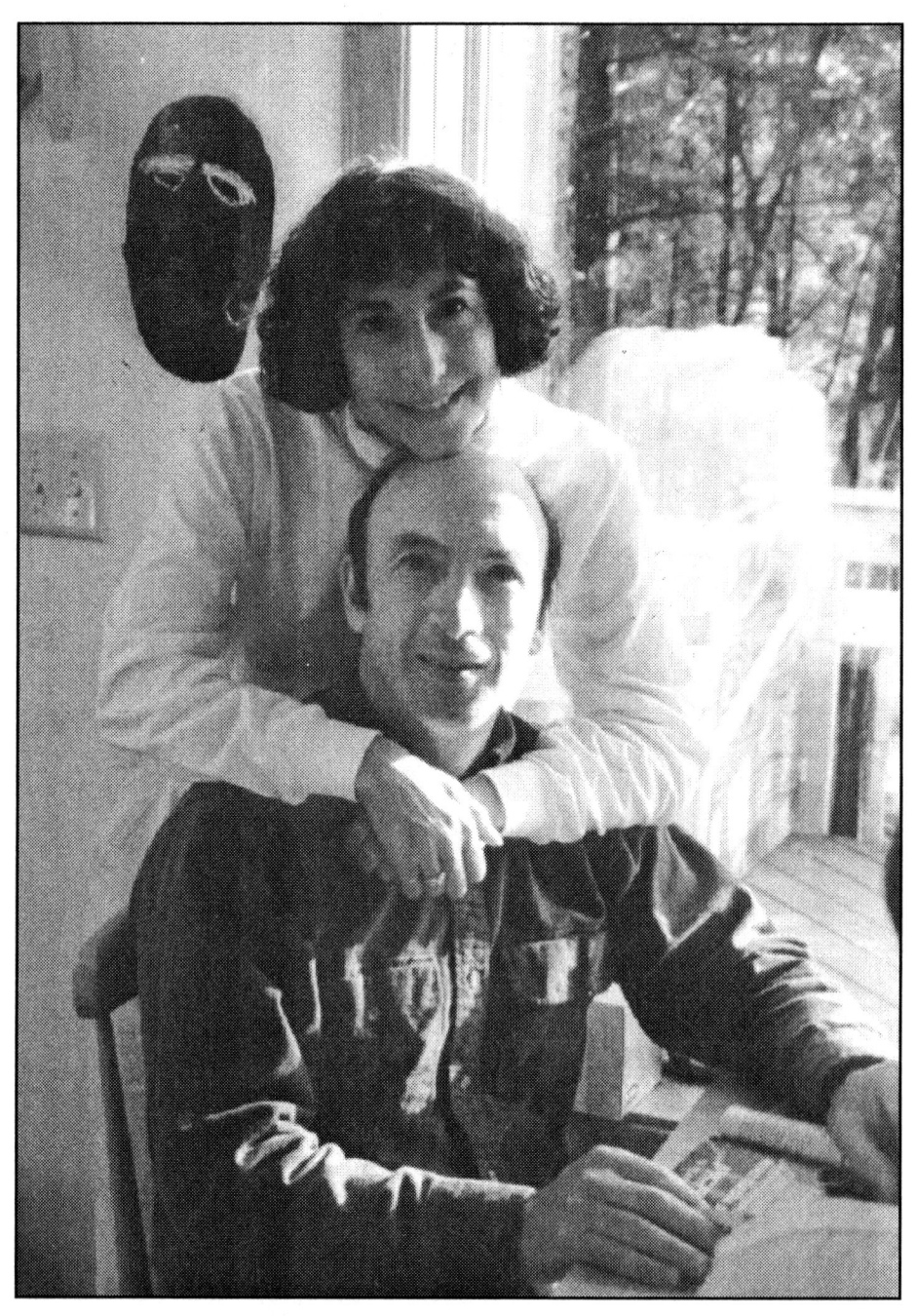

7. My daughter Claire and her husband, Martin Foodman, in their kitchen
(Reading, MA, 1990)

8. My son, Dan, with his wife, Cassandra, at their wedding reception (New York City, 1996)

EQUAL PAY

Dad sues NBC in landmark court case

Paula Kassell

Question: Why do hardly any fathers take time off from their jobs to take care of their children. **Answer**: Corporate policies.

Policy No. 1. Paying women so much less than men that it doesn't make sense for the father to stay home while the mother returns to work after giving birth.

Policy No. 2. Granting women maternity leaves with job security but refusing men paternity leaves altogether or granting them without job security.

Policy No. 3. Standard workplace attitudes: "Job first, family second: Can a man be gung ho for advancement if he wants to stay home to raise a baby?"

Even in Sweden, where paid parental leave for fathers as well as mothers has been legislated since 1974, fathers account for only about 20 percent of the time taken (and a fifth of them stay home no more than nine days). This is because Sweden has one of the most segregated job markets in Europe, with women in the lower paying jobs. "Studies show that the higher her salary, the greater chance that the father will use his share of the paid parental leave of absence," Birgitta Wistrand reported in her recent book, **Swedish Women on the Move**. Psychological attitudes are important, too, in a Swedish father's decision. If there are male colleagues at work who have previously taken paternity leave, this is an important positive influence, Wistrand noted.

A first-time-ever court case in New York City is bringing all these factors into focus. Richard Batsche, an engineer who has worked for NBC for 14 years, applied for a six-week unpaid leave last August to take care of his baby while his wife, a TWA flight attendant, was away on duty. NBC agreed to the leave but refused to guarantee his job or seniority rights. In January he filed a class action suit in Federal court and a sex discrimination complaint with the Federal Equal Employment Opportunity Commission (EEOC) against NBC and also against his union. The union contract calls for up to six months maternity leave for women with guaranteed job and seniority security.

Nevertheless, the union, Local 11 of the National Association of Broadcast Employees and Technicians (NABET), is on Batsche's side, said Arthur Kent, its president. The crux of the issue to Kent is "that an individual who has the right to take a leave should be given that leave with the guarantee of getting the job back, regardless of the reason for the leave. We are still in this case with both our feet and will join Batsche in the case at EEOC or anyplace else," Kent insisted. "It very well might be that the wording of the contract needs to be changed," Kent said, although a letter to the company from the union's international president served notice in 1979 that the wording of the contract should be considered gender-free.

As we go to press the status of the court case is as follows: On Jan. 27, Judge Mary Johnson Lowe of the Federal district court in Manhattan dismissed Batsche's suit, ruling the court lacked jurisdiction, but without ruling on the merits of the case. The proper forum, she said is the EEOC, where Batsche has already filed a complaint. Richard F. Bellman, Batsche's attorney, has appealed Judge Lowe's denial of a preliminary injunction to force NBC to grant him an immediate leave while his suit is pending.

Bellman bases the charge of sex discrimination on the clear distinction made between **a disability leave for childbirth** (under the union contract this is up to 12 weeks with pay) and **an additional leave for maternity reasons** (given to females under the contract for up to six months without pay but with job security). Bellman told **New Directions for Women**: "We say that six months really is not a disability provision. It also involves child-rearing. We say that it's discriminatory not to give male employees equal access to that privilege."

THE BATSCH FAMILY

NBC gave **New Directions for Women** a two-sentence response to inquiries: "NBC's paternity and maternity leave policies are consistent with legal requirements. There is no merit to this complaint." This of course provides no insight into NBC's interest in maintaining such a policy.

One of its main rivals, CBS, offers maternity and paternity leaves that are exactly the same, including job security. The Ford Foundation, Procter and Gamble and AT&T are other companies that provide paternity leaves, though a 1981 survey of corporations by Catalyst turned up only 9 percent that do, while 96 percent offer maternity benefits. Other companies, such as IBM and Equitable Life, grant leaves for "personal needs" for up to a year or two without having a specific paternity leave policy.

What happened at AT&T might prove to be a forecast of the ultimate outcome of the NBC case, forced or voluntary. In 1978 the ACLU Women's Rights Project filed a complaint on behalf of Bill Spoerri, an AT&T employee who wanted a child care leave to care for his new son. He was granted a six month leave but without the guarantee of re-employment, though pregnant women could get up to a year's leave with guaranteed job rights.

On April 29, 1979, the effective date of the federal Pregnancy Discrimination Act, AT&T changed its policy and made child care leaves available on a gender-neutral basis, with a comparable position guaranteed for up to six months.

Only a few men at AT&T have taken advantage of this policy, Catalyst reported in May 1981. "The men who have taken the leave tend to be earning less than their wives," commented Liz Simonski, who works in AT&T's benefits department.

The whole situation points up how corporate policies lock us into traditional sex roles—to such an extent that no man has ever brought this issue to court before.

© 1982 Paula Kassell

EQUAL PAY

Going underground has its pitfalls

Paula Kassell

One of the surest routes to equal pay (read: higher pay) is a blue collar job. Ronnie Zuhlke is a coal miner. She earns $9.50 an hour working 500 feet underground at Bethlehem Steel's Marianna Mine in Carnegie, PA.

In the two years since she started going down into the mine, she has progressed through three job levels. In the bottom-rated job, bratticing, she hung canvas over the coal-mining machine to control the dust. This job required picking up 50-pound bags of rock dust. Respirators are supplied free by the company, she said, though not required by law; but employees do not wear them because they are cumbersome.

Unwieldy clothing and equipment are a special problem for women miners. A survey on protective equipment conducted by the Coal Employment Project, a non-profit organization started in 1977 to help women get and keep coal-mining jobs, reported that even in 1981 boots and gloves that fit are hard to find, and women end up wearing men's sizes. Then their toes end before the metal safety toe of the boot begins, and the fingers of even the smallest gloves they can find extend over one inch beyond the end of their fingers. One woman lost her hand and a good portion of her arm in a roof-bolting accident: her too-large glove caught in the machine. Hard hats wobble and fall off, leaving the miner in total darkness. Coveralls present the worst dilemma of all. Here is how one woman described it in the CEP survey:

"We do not have porta-potties at our mine. You simply go where you can, when you can... It is difficult when you have to take all your gear off, including your hard-hat, plus coveralls I... do all of the above, then turn out my light... My reasoning is if I see a light coming, they won't see me and I'll be able to act in some way...."

Zuhlke's second job was running the buggy—the shuttle car that picks up the coal from the mining machine and takes it to the railcar or belt. This is better-paying, easier and less physical than bratticing. The third and best job she's had is operating the dumper—mostly pushing buttons as the coal comes off the belt, but a little shoveling is involved.

She also gets three levels of teasing:
• About her political activism and union work ("When are you going to run for president?")
• About sex—sexual teasing "to test my limits and find out what pushes my buttons."
• About competence—her ability to do the job. This did push her buttons, she admitted.

Now that she has worked with the same crew for a long time, some of the men speak up for her if another man makes snide remarks about her competence, and to make sure she gets her turn to run the buggy. One of her particular buddies is a man who has been in the mine 14 years. There is one other woman on her crew who has been in the mine for five years. Her crew ranges in age from 24 to 56. She is 33.

One day a new mechanic in her crew tacked up several pictures of naked women in the rest area. She took them down and felt that most of the men understood why, though nobody openly supported her. Two days later, more pictures appeared. The next day the pictures were down. Of course the men suspected her, but the rumor spread that a black preacher working on an earlier shift tore them down. They have never gone up again. Zuhlke is lucky that this is the most flagrant incident she has to report.

At the Second National Conference of Women Coal Miners in 1980, sexual harassment emerged as one of their major problems. A 1981 survey by the Coal Employment Project showed that a majority had been subjected to harassment in some form from supervisors, co-workers or union officials. An outrageous 53 percent of the respondents reported being propositioned by their supervisors: "He told me if I played along with him I wouldn't have to shovel belt. I didn't play so I ended up shoveling half the belts in the mines." The Coal Employment Project and the Coal Mining Women's Support Team have since jointly published a brochure, **Sexual Harassment in the Mines: Legal Rights, Legal Remedies.**

Zuhlke's Marianna Mine employs a relatively high proportion of women—about 5 percent. She enjoys the camaraderie among the women that this affords and takes pleasure in watching the other women bid for higher jobs.

According to the records, a total of 3,556 women have commenced underground mining careers in this country since the first woman was hired in West Virginia in 1973. By 1979 more than 1,000 women were working as miners. In 1981, women were 9.2 percent of the new miners hired that year, up from 8.7 percent for 1980. But the numbers are small—261 women hired in 1981 (a strike year with few hires) and 355 women in 1980.

Ronnie Zuhlke feels that most of the men in the mine do accept women as co-workers. Men understand that women are also supporting families, and they are well aware that as secretaries or waitresses women would be earning $450 to $500 a month in mining country, while as coal miners they are earning $450 a week.

"And," Zuhlke points out, "if I can do it, any woman can who wants to can." Zuhlke is 5 foot 4 inches tall and weighs 110 pounds.

For more information: Coal Employment Project & Coal Mining Women's Support Team, P.O. Box 3403, Oak Ridge, TN 37830; telephone (615) 482-3428. The Fourth National Conference of Women Miners (open to women who are not miners) is June 25-27 at Kentucky Wesleyan College, Owensboro, KY.

(c) 1982 Paula Kassell

Artist-inventor-activist wrapped up in one suffragist

Paula Kassell

Blanche Ames' life encompassed more than art for art's sake. The first major exhibition of her art and life, at the Brockton (MA) Art Museum capsulized this idea: Blanche Ames, Artist and Activist.

Its recent appearance at the Brockton Art Museum is not surprising. The director is a woman, Marilyn Friedman Hoffman, who describes the museum as "committed to the research and exhibition of the works of historic American women artists as well as artists from the Brockton area." Ames was born in Lowell in 1878 and the home she established with her husband, now Borderland State Park, is in North Easton, MA.

The core of the show was 75 paintings, drawings, cartoons and family photographs. But here life was illustrated by the artifacts representing her other accomplishments, together with the show catalog's detailed descriptions and explanations of how they fit in with her paintings.

Blanche and her brother, Adelbert, developed theories of depth perception that she used to give a sense of depth to a flat canvas by blurring or sharpening the edges of objects and by using blues and light colors in the background. The contrast between the objects out of focus heightened the emphasis on the clearly delineated subject, creating an illusion of depth.

Most interesting are her woman suffrage cartoons and her life as an active feminist since her days at Smith College, where she graduated as president of her class in 1899. When she married Oakes Ames (same surname as her's, no relation), an equally ardent proponent of women's rights, he suggested foregoing wedding rings, recognizing them as a sign of bondage.

By 1914 she was an officer in the Massachusetts Woman Suffrage League. (Oakes chaired the campaign committee of the Men's League for Women Suffrage.) Her suffrage cartoons done in 1915 appeared in local and national newspapers, coming to the attention of President Taft. He called the implications of the cartoon, Meanwhile We Drown, "absurd and unjust to opponents of suffrage."

In 1916 Blanche Ames co-founded the Birth Control League of Massachusetts. She devised a contraceptive device using a baby's teething ring or Mason jar sealing ring to make a diaphragm and developed a formula for spermicide.

That was only one of her inventions. She also invented a hexagonal lumber cutter to minimize waste and in 1941, in response to the wartime threat of aircraft, developed a rope and wire contraption to ensnare low-flying airplanes. In 1968, the year before she died at the age of 91, she was the co-inventor of an anti-pollution device for toilets.

Meanwhile They Drown, 1915 suffrage cartoon by Blanche Ames.

Blanche Ames, throughout her long career as an artist, aimed at honest, straightforward depiction of face and nature. This enjoyable exhibit was a document of her success.

The 36-page catalogue, prepared for the show by Bonnie L. Crane of the museum's curatorial staff. The catalogue is available by mail from the Brockton Art Museum, Oak Street, Brockton, MA 02401 for $5.76 postpaid.

EQUAL PAY

Child Care ignored

Paula Kassell

There is a bright, bright spot in the otherwise/gloomy child care picture. The glow emanates from Freeport, TX, where Intermedics, a manufacturer of medical products including a cardiac pacemaker, operates a child care center for 292 employees' children.

During its first year—it opened in November 1979—the company experienced 15,000 fewer hours of absenteeism in its manufacturing department, a predominantly female workforce that at the same time grew from 150 to 300 employees.

From the beginning, the child care center contributed mightily to recruiting both production line and professional women AND men. Alice Duncan, the center director, told New Directions for Women.

Turnover decreased 23 percent during the first year and an additional 37 percent the second year, for a total overall decrease of 60 percent, she said.

Intermedics' A.B. Beutel II Child Care Center is named for the company president who initiated it. He was killed in a helicopter accident before the center opened. It sits in a new 15,600 square foot building on the main road to the plant, about three miles away. It was set up as a wholly-owned subsidiary serving employees children only, and operates at a loss. Employees pay $15 per week per child. The children of about 20 percent of Intermedics 1,500 employees are enrolled, with a waiting list of 175.

The company is building a new plant 30 miles from Freeport which will include a 35,000 square foot center for over 500 children.

The rest of the news about child care is mostly bad.

EXAMPLE: The Shawneetown, IL Day Care Center managed to get by with the help of a CETA employee. But when federal budget cuts terminated the CETA job, the center had to fold. This is the result, as told by Rep. Paul Simon of Illinois: The former CETA employee is now drawing unemployment compensation, along with the four women who were full-time employees of the center. Four women who were able to work because the center cared for their children have had to quit their jobs and go on welfare. The bottom line, as totted up by Simon: one CETA employee's salary saved, and nine people added to the unemployment compensation and welfare rolls.

Since the early days of the women's movement, feminist rhetoric has put forth child care as a right of women and families, pointing at the European model, where most governments provide it as public expense. But between 1971, when President Nixon vetoed a comprehensive child care bill, up to 1979, when the latest, watered down federal bill was defeated, this demand has been a dead end and child care has been a lost issue.

So lost that neither the Bureau of Labor Statistics nor the Census Bureau is collecting data. The latest word on child care arrangements of working families (How many children in centers? How many with relatives? How many with paid baby-sitters? How many latch key children?) are 1975 figures published in October 1979. The 1980 census asked no questions about child care arrangements.

So lost that no one knows how many child care center slots there are in the United States (the latest figures are for 1976-77).

What we do know is the size of the problem:

• 2,299,000 single-woman households with children under 6-years-old (March 1980 figure for never married, husband absent, widowed, divorced.)

• 6,933,000 working women with children under six—in fact, 48.9 percent of working women have children under six (March 1981 figures). And that says nothing about working women with young school-age children.

A problem that size will not go away if we continue to overlook it; it is, instead growing larger daily. By 1990, forecasts have said, there will be 7,519,000 working women with children under six; however, this figure already appears far too low.

Can we afford to ignore their needs?

Information sources: Statistics or lack thereof—Bureau of Labor Statistics, US Department of Labor; US Census Bureau. Forecast—The Subtle Revolution: Women at Work edited by Ralph E. Smith (The Urban Institute) 1979.

© 1982 Paula Kassell

EQUAL PAY

Latch key children's needs a pressing problem

Paula Kassell

We know that the number of child care centers for preschool children are totally inadequate to meet our needs (see Equal Pay, July/August 1982). Programs for school-age children in the late afternoon hours and on school holiday and vacation days are much, much rarer.

It's a disaster for our youngsters who are roaming the streets or at home alone watching TV.

It's a disaster for the mothers who have to settle for whatever part-time or part-year jobs we can get in order to accommodate the school clock and calendar. Many women purposely and willingly structure their lives to be full-time homemakers until their youngest child goes to school, not realizing that even then they will probably not be free to pursue a full-time career of their choice.

There is grassroots activity across the country to solve this problem and it may turn out to be the hidden issue of the mid-80s, following child abuse and incest into the public consciousness at what our society does to our children.

• The Wellesley College Center for Research on Women (Wellesley, MA) set up a School-Age Child Care Project in 1979 to find out what's going on and to help others get started. They have discovered child care activity at public schools here and there around the country, said Mickey Seltzer, the director, almost all of it instigated and administered by parent or community groups, not by the schools, even though school sites are used for the programs.

The Wellesley project has a book coming out in late September designed to foster a groundswell of activity: School-Age Child Care: An Action Manual. The actions are geared to parents, schools and social service agencies, with examples and anecdotes drawn from demonstration projects in eight communities.

The program should be recreational rather than tutorial, the book will advise, though a request for help with homework from a student should not be turned down. Arts and crafts, sports and trips are suggested. The children learn to work with each other and have a chance to talk to adults in an unhurried atmosphere. Taken for granted in any material coming out of the Wellesley center is stress on training the staff to plan a non-sexist, non-racist curriculum.

• The University of North Carolina Center for Early Adolescent (Carrboro, NC) is concentrating on the young adolescent—aged 10 to 15, roughly those in fifth through ninth grades. Leah Lefstein, the center's associate director, calls them "the most misunderstood children in America." So the center surveyed parents and the kids themselves about the after-school programs they want.

Soon the center will publish a book, 3:00 to 6:00 pm: Young Adolescents at Home and in the Community, due in September, addressed to policy makers, youth workers and parents. The book will cover social, physical and intellectual development during early adolescence, addressing the question, "What assumptions are we making that we should not?" Lefstein said.

An important chapter covers The Children's Time Study, and investigation of 10-to13-year-olds in Oakland, CA. This study addresses the question, "Are these children depending on community facilities now in danger of shutting down because of budget cuts?" "At the very time there are fewer adults at home, libraries are reducing their hours, playgrounds are losing supervisors and bus lines are shutting down," Lefstein pointed out.

The last two chapters of the book will cover funding sources and give a preliminary overview of programs that now exist all over the country. A bibliography and resource list is included.

• Dr. Lynette Long of Loyola College, Baltimore, and Dr. Thomas Long of Catholic University, Washington, DC also went directly to the source for their forthcoming book on latch key children, those children who are left to fend for themselves while a parent or parents are at work. They did nationwide interviews of parents of latch key children and adults who were former latch key children, then interviewed latch key children themselves in the Baltimore-Washington area. The study, of course, uncovered fears, feelings of isolation and loneliness, and absenteeism among those who had to get themselves ready for school in the morning—they missed the bus, missed breakfast, or grabbed junk food.

But some former latch key children, looking back, said they had benefitted—they had independence, freedom to do what they wanted, closer ties with their sisters and brothers.

The book the Longs, a wife-husband team, are just starting to write will be called Preparing Your Child for Self-Care; A Handbook for Parents. It is about children aged 6 to 12.

That's one necessary and realistic approach to the problem of latch key children, given today's official climate of neglect for human needs. It is not the solution parents want. The Center for Early Adolescence found most working parents "frantic," according to Leah Lefstein, "What they want for their children is "constant adult supervision."

For further information about publication dates and prices of the forthcoming books (not available at press time):

School-Age Child Care: An Action Manual (due late September). School-Age Child Care Project, Wellesley College Center for Research on Women, 828 Washington, St., Wellesley, MA 02181; (617) 431-1453.

3:00 to 6:00 pm: Young Adolescents at Home and in the Community (due early September). Anne Richardson, Publications Manager, Center for Early Adolescence of University of North Carolina at Chapel Hill, Suite 223, Carr Mill Mall, Carrboro, NC 27510; (919) 966-1148.

Preparing Your Child for Self-Care; A Handbook for Parents (due Spring 1983). Dr. Thomas Long, Catholic University of America, 620 Michigan Ave., NE, Washington, DC 20064; (202) 635-5800.

©1982 Paula Kassell

Politicians beware!

This year feminists and feminist organizations were more active in national, state and local political campaigns than in any previous election—a sign of growing political maturity in the women's movement.

"Are you only for women candidates, or will feminists throw their weight behind male candidates who support women's issues?" we used to be asked. This year we gave a resounding answer, fundraising and working for several men, particularly the re-election of Lowell Weicker, our friend in the Senate.

The Senate campaign in New Jersey posed the toughest problem. Millicent Fenwick, an advocate for feminist issues, first in the New Jersey State Assembly and then in the House of Representatives, had been our ideal of a woman candidate since the early 1970s. This year, however, many women looked beyond the feminist issues. This year the economic well-being of our nation and our people became to many of us the most important feminist issue of all.

Authoritative studies recently reported show that **every 1 percent increase in unemployment** brought a 2 percent increase in cardiovascular deaths, a 5 to 6 percent increase in homicides, a 5 percent increase in imprisonment, a 3 to 4 percent increase in first admissions to mental hospitals and about a 5 to 6 percent increase in infant mortality. We might not have been aware of the statistics, but we have certainly been experiencing the misery that unemployment visits on the whole family.

It was on the economic issues that many women reluctantly abandoned Fenwick: she had voted down the line for the Reagan program and budget cuts, even though they devastated the economic and social support systems that are so important to women and families, especially to the poor. Fenwick is also tainted by the Republican Party—the party that opposes the Equal Rights Amendment, that is working to deny us legal abortions, that is failing to enforce the laws against discrimination, that is against affirmative action.

Running against Millicent Fenwick was Frank Lautenberg, a political unknown who made a 100 percent feminist score in his answers to our campaign questionnaire on the issues. The National Organization for Women endorsed Lautenberg. The National Women's Political Caucus and the Women's Campaign Fund supported Fenwick.

When the voting booth curtains closed behind us on election day and we were alone with our consciences, those of us who were about to vote for Fenwick and those of us who were about to vote for Lautenberg were equally distressed.

But we have all reached a new plateau of political maturity and gained the respect of both parties. Forevermore we will work and vote and upset apple carts until the entire Congress is on our side and not one member will dare to vote to balance the budget on the backs of women and children and families and the poor and unfortunate.

Paula Kassell

EQUAL PAY

Hospitals may fill gap in child care

Paula Kassell

In 1971 when I was vice-president of the Dover (NJ) Child Care Center, we tried and failed to convince Dover General Hospital to give us the use of a house it had just bought across the street from the hospital. We needed to expand our space to accommodate more children of hospital employees and from the community. Dover General still does not have a child care center.

It is bucking a "whole bonanza going on because of greater competition for employees within the health care field." That is the way Mark Podolner, director of the Lake View Child Care Center in Chicago, described the rush to open centers at hospitals—from 75 across the country in 1978 to about 200 in 1982, many of them new and more of them in the works.

Interest is so high that Podolner is working toward forming a new National Association of Hospital Child Care Directors. Hospitals have almost as many child care programs as all other employers combined, according to Sandy Burud, project manager of the National Employer-Supported Child Care Project. She says there have been child care centers in hospitals since the Civil War because hospitals have always had a recruitment problem and a largely female workforce.

There are many reasons why a hospital is the ideal location for a child care center:

• It may be the only facility in a town or rural area that is used as a matter of course by everyone regardless of sex, race, religion and economic level. Hospital employees themselves run the same gamuts.

• Food, laundry and cleaning services are available, reducing the staff required for the center.

• Routine and emergency medical care is right on the premises.

• Caring for infants is taken for granted.

• All hospitals are 24-hour, seven-day operations geared to shifts.

• Hospitals are usually centrally located in areas served by public transportation.

It is disappointing to find, therefore, that while a minority of hospital child care centers are open to children from the community whose parents are not hospital employees, many are not. "It's hard enough to find space just for employees," said Sister Anne Lorraine Mahlmeister of St. Mary's Hospital and Health Center in Tucson, who has visited centers around the country in the process of researching whether St. Mary's should start one. Another reason is that hospitals can get Medicare reimbursement for caring for employees' children—the center is considered an expense of running the hospital.

Money is the root of two other serious problems stressed by Mark Podolner that will be on the agenda when the hospital child care directors and other hospital administrators meet in November:

• "Are we serving an elite?" is one of the questions they are facing. Weekly fees per child are so high that only doctors, nurses and technicians can afford to send their children, so the economic and class mixture of hospital employees is not reflected in the children enrolled in the child care center. At Podolner's Lake View Center in Chicago, which was started six years ago as a joint community and hospital venture, fees are $50 per week per child for hospital employees and $55 for others. Enrollment is about half and half. Laundry, kitchen and other such employees, a huge percentage of the hospital staff, cannot afford it, he admits, pointing out that actual costs are close to $100 per week per child, so the hospital is actually subsidizing about 50 percent

• Pay inequity (and the lawsuits that can result) is the other problem on Podolner's mind. Though he believes salaries paid to hospital child care workers are better than at other centers, he recognizes they are "much lower" than for other professional hospital employees. "It is pretty standard," he said, "for child care employees to be paid significantly below their grade or to be graded in the same or lower levels than the hospital's sanitation workers (laundry, kitchen, etc.) or untrained people."

Sen. Paula Hawkins (R-FL) is drafting legislation for federal matching grants to hospitals to help them start new centers. Priority will be given to 24-hour, seven-day programs. Some hospitals have even asked that dependent elderly be served as well as children, because many nurses are responsible for elderly relatives. She plans to introduce the bill in this lame duck session of Congress and is soliciting comments, especially from nurses, so that a final bill can be introduced next year.

For further information and to comment:

Child Care: The New Business Tool. A complete how-to manual for employers and employers investigating the feasibility of child care programs; covers all kinds of employer-supported child care, not just on-site centers—voucher payments, resource referral, summer camps for school-age children, and other services. (due early 1983, price not available at press time). Sandy Burud, project manager, National Employer-Supported Child Care Project, Child Care Information Service, 363 East Villa, Pasadena, CA 91109; (213) 796-4341.

National Association of Hospital Child Care Directors, c/o Mark Podolner, Lake View Child Care Center, 900 West Oakdale, Chicago, IL 60657; (312) 883-7051.

Sen. Paula Hawkins, Senate Office Building, Washington, DC 20510; (202) 224-3041.

©1982 Paula Kassell

EQUAL PAY

Discrimination in marketplace a reality

Paula Kassell

If you could raise children and sell them at a profit, child care workers would be paid as much as (maybe more than?) cattle breeders. But since children bring no money in the marketplace, the minimum wage, more or less, is the prevailing wage for child care.

That is the ultimate meaning of the prevailing wage argument against the concept of equal pay for work of comparable worth. The argument goes like this: "The marketplace should determine what employers will pay for each type of work, according to supply and demand. Why would any employer offer higher pay scales to nurses, for instance, when sufficient employees (women) accept and keep jobs at lower rates? Likewise, the higher pay offered for other jobs, such as tree trimmer, is explained by the difficulty of finding enough employees (men) to fill the available jobs."

The argument is absurd.

First, the law of supply and demand, which is after all only theoretical, works only in a perfectly free market place. The very idea of offering pay based on prevailing wages constrains the freedom of the market, making it work more like a monopoly. This is how.

Employers study other companies to determine what the prevailing wages are for each job:

• For clerical and factory jobs, some companies do their own surveys. Local and regional personnel associations and chambers of commerce often collect information on prevailing wages in their area and distribute it to their members or sell it. The US Department of Labor regularly publishes earnings data in detail.

• Surveying professional levels is more complicated, but the American Management Association does it and makes the results available for purchase by members and nonmembers. The National Science Foundation, the National Research Council and the Scientific Manpower Commission, plus many professional associations such as the American Chemical Society also compile data about salaries in different disciplines and in different settings—and by sex.

Second, if wages move according to supply and demand, why haven't nurses' salaries risen high enough to combat the dangerous shortage of nurses in hospitals? Why are registered nurses leaving their profession to take higher paying jobs? Supply and demand is obviously not working.

Third, a system that assigns wage rates without regard to the education, training and responsibility required for each job is absurd on its very face. Working for the State of California, I reported in 1979, a clerk typist needed a high school education, knowledge of office machines and equipment, grammar, spelling and so forth. A warehouse worker needed the ability to read and write English; no other educational or special skills. Warehouse workers, just about all male, made $199 more per month than clerk typists, 97 percent female. This kind of discrepancy is still fashionable today.

Upsetting that finely tuned discriminatory marketplace is "pregnant with the possibility of disrupting the entire economic system of the United States of America . . . I am not going to do it." That's quoted from the ruling of the judge in the first and most famous court case on comparable worth, brought in 1976 by nurses employed by city and county hospitals in Denver to protest that men trimming trees on the hospital grounds were being paid more than graduate nurses caring for patients in the hospital beds. The nurses lost that case all the way, when the Supreme Court declined to review. The concept of comparable worth was rejected after the judge conceded that the nurses had proved their contention of a discriminatory market place.

Had the judges and justices forgotten that disruption of the economy was used as an argument against both the minimum wage and the Equal Pay Act? And giving women the right to vote was supposed to upset all of society (I'm still hoping).

Since the Denver nurses' case the courts have edged closer to the idea of comparable worth. In 1981, in the Gunther case, brought by jail matrons, the Supreme Court went so far as to find the scope of Title VII of the 1964 Civil Rights Act much broader than the 1963 Equal Pay Act, saying that discrimination claims brought under Title VII are not restricted to claims for equal pay for "substantially equal work."

That's an important statement because, though almost everybody believes in equal pay for equal work, there is hardly any such thing as equal work. The Equal Pay Act enforces equal pay only where women and men work side by side doing the same work. But that is rare. Most jobs are men's jobs (and hardly any women hold them) or women's jobs (and hardly any men hold them).

So women are now working toward the new goal: EQUAL PAY FOR WORK OF EQUAL VALUE. This is called "pay equity" or "comparable worth" or "equal pay for work of comparable value." They all mean the same thing—giving women's jobs full credit for the education, training, experience and responsibilities they require.

At the first Conference on Pay Equity back in October 1979, Eleanor Holmes Norton, then head of the federal Equal Employment Opportunity Commission, described it as "the issue of the '80s—a true sleeping giant." That giant must be awakened.

This is the fifth EQUAL PAY column on the comparable worth issue. Previous columns were **Separate and not equal in the workplace** (Spring 1979), **Comparable worth** (Autumn 1979), **Prevailing wages** (Winter 1979-80), and **Comparable worth on firing line** (March/April 1981).

For additional information:

Comparable Worth Project, 488 41 St., No. 5, Oakland, CA 94609; telephone (415) 658-1808. Catalog of publication: $3. Quarterly newsletter: $16 institutions; $8 individuals; $4 low income.

Equal Pay for Work of Comparable Worth: An Annotated Bibliography, published and distributed by American Library Association, Office for Library Personnel Resources, 50 East Huron St., Chicago, Il 60611. $4.

Copyright 1982 Paula Kassell

EQUAL PAY

Unemployment rates deceiving

Paula Kassell

The bare facts on unemployment rates show women a little better off than men:

adult women	9.2%	adult men	10.1%
white women	8.1%	white men	9.2%
black women	16.5%	black men	20.5%

You have to delve deeper into the statistics to reveal the whole picture:

- Women who maintain families suffer an unemployment rate of 13.2 percent. This group "has had a sharp increase in unemployment during this recession," said Samuel Ehrenhalt, regional commissioner for the US Bureau of Labor Statistics.
- "Discouraged" workers, most of whom are women, Ehrenhalt told New Directions for Women, increased from 1.2 million to 1.85 million in the past year, rising by 300,000 in the last quarter alone. They are not counted in the labor force (and therefore do not figure in the unemployment rates) because they are not looking for work. As Ehrenhalt pointed out, many women who might want to enter the work force do not even try to do so because the job market is not expanding.
- Then there are the "involuntary underemployed," those working less than full time because of slack work or because part-time work is the only work they can find.

The lower unemployment rate compared to men that women are experiencing these days is a reversal of the situation New Directions for Women uncovered in 1972 and 1973. At that time we were a statewide newspaper and, at our insistence, the New Jersey Department of Labor and Industry compiled unemployment rates by sex for the first time, revealing wide differences between the rates. The month of September 1973 was typical, with 5.0 percent unemployment for men and 8.4 percent for women.

WE CONTINUE TO HAVE CONFIDENCE IN OUR ECONOMIC PLAN!

Ehrenhalt calls our present situation "a blue collar recession," with men's unemployment rising faster than women's while stereotypical female jobs remain more stable. In fact, for several years jobs in service occupations have been increasing—and in April 1982 gained the majority over industrial production jobs (manufacturing, construction and mining) for the first time in US economic history. Health services alone added 235,000 jobs, upping the total to 5,717,000. Accounting service jobs also increased significantly; Ehrenhalt singled out this profession to note that today 40 percent of accountants are women, though 20 years ago there were few women accountants.

The new opportunities are just the ones that have accounted for over 90 percent of the net increase in the number of jobs held by women in the 70s—transportation, public utilities, trade, finance, insurance, real estate, services and government. The largest occupational group in the nation today is clerical; it used to be blue collar.

All these facts and trends seem favorable to women, at least on the surface. But, again, you have to delve deeper to reveal the whole picture. Roberta McKay, an economist with the Women's Bureau of the US Department of Labor, sees an ominous possibility on the horizon.

At present, we all know, women are taking few jobs from men. Despite the advance of a significant number of women into a few fields, and the token advance of a few women into most fields, on the whole, women and men hold totally different jobs. Ending this sex-segregated job market by integrating women into the higher paying men's jobs has always been our aim, considered a prime means of closing the earnings gap. Yet two-way traffic—integrating men into women's jobs—seemed an absurd possibility. Why would men push their way into low-paying, dead-end women's work?

Now Roberta McKay is speculating that when we come out of the depression, men may be displaced from their usual jobs (in the auto industry, for example). And new technologies will enable fewer people to run larger and larger factories. Growth, on the other hand, is predicted to continue in the old (clerical) and new (computer) fields where women have always found or are newly finding niches. Men may be forced to crowd into women's jobs, McKay speculates, driving wages down even further, and skimming the cream of the best jobs in each field.

That isn't the prospect we had in mind. The only solution for women AND men is an expanding job market. Economic policies that do not quickly lead in that direction are intolerable.

© Copyright 1983 Paula Kassell

"Undercover Story" looks beneath surface

Paula Kassell

We see by the papers that fashionable women are sporting bustles on their derrieres at high-society functions. Even these women have fallen for the current back-side craze (see any jeans ad).

Soon fashion interest will no doubt shift to obsession with breasts, legs, crotches (we detect that one already) or waists. The psychologist, J.C. Flugel, was the first to propose a theory of "shifting erogenous zones," Alison Lurie pointed out in **The Language of Clothes**. First one and then another part of the female body is uncovered or focused on and and found exciting.

One of the most debilitating of these fashion crazes was the pursuit of the tiny waist during the second half of the last century and the beginning of the 20th.

"A fashionable woman's corset exerted, on the average, 21 pounds of pressure on her internal organs, and extremes of up to 88 pounds had been measured. (Add to this the fact that a well-dressed woman wore an average of 37 pounds of street clothing in winter months, of which 19 pounds were suspended from her tortured waist.) Some of the short-term results of tight-lacing were shortness of breath, constipation, weakness, and a tendency to violent indigestion. Among the long-term effects were bent or fractured ribs, displacement of the liver, and uterine prolapse (in some cases, the uterus would be gradually forced, by the pressure of the corset, out through the vagina)." (From **For Her Own Good: 150 Years of the Experts' Advice to Women**.)

The advice to women was that corsets were a medical necessity. "Ladies' 'frames,' it was believed, were extremely delicate; their muscles could not hold them up without assistance . . . Well brought up little girls, from the best motives, were laced into juvenile versions of the corset as early as three or four . . . By the time they reached late adolescence they were wearing cages of heavy canvas reinforced with whalebone or steel, and their back muscles had atrophied to the point where they could not sit or stand for long unsupported." (**The Language of Clothes**)

Corsets and other contraptions such as bust suppressors and bust enhancers used over the centuries to force the female anatomy into whatever shape fashion decreed at the moment are the subject of a fascinating show, "The Undercover Story," at the Galleries of the Fashion Institute of Technology in New York, at 27th St. and Seventh Ave. The show will run through May 7 (10 am to 9 pm Tuesday; 10 am to 5 pm Wednesday through Saturday). Admission is free.

Though advertisements and fashion sketches during the tiny-waist mania speak of attaining

Courtesy of the Brooklyn Museum

AMERICAN AND FRENCH corsets from the late 18th through early 20th centuries.

18-inch waist lines, the smallest corsets that have been found have 21-inch circumferences and most corsets of the day squeezed the waist into 24 to 25 inches, said Martha Leopardo, a curator at the Fashion Institute. When, in 1980, the Brooklyn (NY) Museum exhibited 30 corsets dating from 1780 to 1950, Paulette Wilman of the Costume Department explained that waists looked even smaller than they actually were because the corsets plus padding above and below them exaggerated the bust and hips.

A fascinating sidelight to the psychology of women's clothing is that up until the 1850s women wore nothing between their legs. Underpants were frowned upon, Leopardo explained, because they imitated male garments and "they were considered immodest and sexually exciting."

Through all the tortured centuries while women's bodies were supposed to be fat or thin, have large busts or no busts, large hips or no hips, high round bottoms or flat bottoms, dimpled flesh or no cellulite, etc., etc., etc. . . . women have followed fashion's edicts. We still do. Haven't we been made to believe in our hearts that fat is ugly? If next year's fashion arbiters decree tiny waistlines instead of high round buttocks, will we rush to buy corsets like the ones on view at the Fashion Institute?

The Language of Clothes by Alison Lurie (Random House)

For Her Own Good: 150 Years of the Experts' Advice to Women by Barbara Ehrenreich and Deirdre English (Anchor Press/Doubleday)

The Obsession: Reflections on the Tyranny of Slenderness by Kim Chernin (Harper & Row)

Seeing Through Clothes by Anne Hollander (Viking)

Dress for Health: A New Clothes-Consciousness by Maggie Rollo and Stephen B. Nussdorf (Stackpole Books, P.O. Box 1831, Harrisburg, Pa 17105)

IN DEFENSE OF THE FAMILY: Raising Children in America Today by Rita Kramer (Basic Books) $15.50

Paula Kassell

I am not contemptuous of Rita Kramer's ideas and opinions on the family and child-rearing, as she is of my feminist philosophy. And I will not misconstrue her point of view or priorities because I will quote her exactly. "Perhaps it is time to return child care to the home, responsibility to the family, and authority to parents," she states early in the book, following that shortly with "Most of this book is concerned with disproving that statement"; that "child care can be done by anyone." In fact, not even fathers are acceptable: "...they should be cared for by their mothers whenever possible during the earliest years." "Moving into the outside world away from mother, the first person the child encounters is his father. The father has always been there, but usually not a real part of that mother-baby dyad from which the child is hatching."

Her second major position is that children "should not be discouraged from clearly defining themselves as boys or girls with separate patterns of male and female attributes." Using "he" to speak of "the child" throughout the book is completely appropriate in her descriptions, since "he will decide who he is going to be as an emerging adult...what kind of work he will want to do...He accepts the necessity to go out into the world and seek his fortune—find a place for himself and someone of his own."

"Most little girls transfer a good deal of their positive emotion to their fathers around the time they first perceive the difference between the sexes. Then the little girl, too, must make her peace with growing up to be like her mother—instead of actually taking her place—and finding someone she will love and with whom she will have children of her own."

Nothing incites Kramer to ire more than the egalitarian family or any attempt at nonsexist child-rearing. Her most sarcastic comments are directed at Letty Cottin Pogrebin's book, Growing Up Free: Raising Your Child in the 80's (note the similarity of subtitles in the Pogrebin and Kramer books). Kramer writes of Growing Up Free's "ludicrous advocacy of a child-rearing program as repressive as anything in Victorian times in its insistence on standing one extreme on its head to create another one and its humorless advocacy of a constant, unremitting pressure on the child to conform—in this case, to nonconformism." Did she read the same book I did? Here is how Growing Up Free was described in New Directions for Women (March/April 1981) by Ann Martin-Leff, a young mother of an infant: Pogrebin "analyzes the destructive aspects of sexist child-rearing and the beneficial aspects of nonsexist child-rearing: girls and boys who conform rigidly to sex-role stereotypes are usually unhappier than those who don't."

Kramer's third soap box is sex education in the schools. Of course children should be given sex education by their parents. But parents, almost universally, don't. Mary Calderone of the Sex Information and Education Council of the United States (SIECUS), is condemned for developing a curriculum intended to introduce school children to "the varieties of sexual experience" in a "guilt-free atmosphere."

Rita Kramer is proud to be advocating the "family as it has traditionally been defined" (the nuclear male/female pair with children). "For most of us, average middle-class Americans living during the end of the twentieth century," she says, "it is the traditional values of our existing society we want to foster, not subvert, and these are the values we want to transmit to our children...." (Didn't I already read this book in the 1950s? No, really, it is copyright 1983.)

It saddens me that this thoughtful, intelligent woman should be so complacent about our world as it is and has been, and so pessimistic about the possibility of improvement. "There is something dark in human nature that persists," she writes at the end of the book, "whether it is called instinct or sin."

The feminist philosophy, on the other hand, is that we want to raise all our children to be nurturing and caring, not just our daughters, and all our children to be competent and enterprising, not just our sons. Then, when we place the world in their hands, there will be hope for a peaceful, nonviolent, nonpolluted (perhaps even drug-free?) life for the future generations.

Brain gender gap: new mythology

SEX AND THE BRAIN by Jo Durden-Smith and Diane Desimone (Arbor House) $16.95

Paula Kassell

Sex and the Brain ("Gender and the Brain" would be the more accurate title, but "Sex" sells books) is devoted to a popularization of the thesis that male and female hormones cause male and female brains to develop differently. "We (humans) are the creatures, to an extent hitherto unimagined, of biological forces," the authors conclude from their readings and talks with researchers.

By juxtaposing bits and pieces of many people's research and speculations, they tend to add two and two and get five. But they have compiled a great deal of evidence implying, not proving, that the brain hemispheres of women and men are differently organized: Male left hemispheres develop more slowly (possibly due to the male hormone, testosterone, causing learning disorders, especially language disorders such as dyslexia, plus autism, stuttering, aphasia and perhaps also hyperactivity and even schizophrenia and left-handedness. Testosterone is also connected to another brain behavior—aggression. Female brains have greater communication between the hemispheres and provide for superior verbal and communication skills, emotional and social sophistication—and intuition.

And of course we could not have a book on male/female brain differences without a go at mathematical ability. The researchers cited, Camilla Persson Benbow and Julian Stanley of John Hopkins, concluded: "we favor the hypothesis that sex differences in achievement in and attitude towards mathematics result from superior male mathematical ability, which may in turn be related to greater male ability in spatial tasks."

The trouble with the Benbow Stanley study is that they "were looking for gifted seventh- and eighth-graders—twelve-year-olds, basically . . ." But that is exactly the age when girls begin to suppress their abilities that push them to compete with and surpass boys. It is the intellectual equivalent of not beating the boys at tennis. Benbow told the authors that she would love to have pointed out to her an environmental difference overlooked in their study. She obviously has no idea that a 12-year-old girl is living in an entirely different social, psychological and emotional environment than a 12-year-old boy.

More important than the very small statistical differences between the sexes in some aspects of math such as problem solving ability is the large degree of overlap between the two groups—many girls surpassing many boys. The subject of sex differences in mathematical abilities is extremely controversial. Sex and the Brain presents a one-sided view.

Almost all the differences between male and female brains hinted at in Sex and the Brain lead to the conclusion that females excel males in the attributes we need today to correct all the tragedies foisted on the world by the male attributes over the past millenia. Who wants to think more like a man?

But beware! If, in the 19th century, scientists had discovered that men's brains were smaller than women's, they no doubt would have announced: "Smaller brains permit faster thinking, and therefore men's brains are superior to women's." What did they say when they found men's brains to be larger? "Women's smaller brains make them incapable of intellectual work."

We are the sex that has within our bodies the marvelous apparatus to manufacture and then feed a new human. Yet we are told that we envy the appendage dangling in front of men. If that difference between the sexes can be used to call females disadvantaged, any difference can.

That's why my usual reaction to a new "biology is destiny" campaign is to mount up and ride into battle.

EQUAL PAY

Times' progress 'woefully inadequate'

Paula Kassell

One particular sex discrimination suit—the suit against The New York Times-is important for women far beyond the world of journalism. The people who work at The Times are responsible for setting policies and starting trends that affect the way news is reported in other newspapers and on television througout the world.

Until women-owned, women-run publications like **New Directions for Women** can develop circulation in the millions, most women must depend on overwhelmingly male-owned, male-run media for the information that we get about each other and our issues. Indeed, until news organs, including The New York Times, stop depriving themselves of the full use of the female talent pool, they will not be as good as they could be. The men who run The Times say that, themselves, but too many of them have been unable or unwilling to outgrow the traditional macho chauvinism of the newsroom.

In November 1978, The New York Times finally capitulated and agreed to an out-of-court settlement of the discrimination suit brought by a number of its women employees in 1974. In addition to back pay awards, The Times pledged to place significant numbers of women in every news and commercial department of the newspaper, and specific percentage goals were set for all job categories. The settlement was a four-year affirmative action plan that set goals right up to the top corporate offices (see "Times settlement 'unprecedented,'" Winter 1978-79 issue).

The unfinished history of this suit is worthy of study. The consent decree has now lapsed—the report on 1982 hires and female/male ratios in every job category is the company's final reporting obligation to The Times Women's Caucus enforceable by court action, according to Harriet Rabb, the attorney who represented the employees in the suit. But the caucus can still question the result.

As of this writing, the caucus is studying its options for pursuing the goals it sees as not met during the settlement period, including the possibility of going back into court. The Times' position, stated by its publisher, Arthur Ochs Sulzberger, at the 1983 shareholders meeting in April, is that they have met the requirements of the suit.

During the four-year period covered by the settlement, The Times has indeed placed many women in positions of responsibility, in the news departments and in business management, that in the past were closed to them. But the results are uneven. What bothers the caucus, says Emily Weiner, caucus committee coordinator, is the "woefully inadequate" record of hires in some important news and business job categories "dealing with infuence and power."

The Times own reports bear this out: in one job category on the business side that includes high management positions there has actually been a decline in the number of women over the four years:

1979	16.7 percent women
1980	12.5 percent women
1981	9. percent women
1982	8. percent women

The goal agreed to in the settlement was that at the end of the four years 20 percent of the population in these decision-making positions would be women.

The New York Times masthead reveals that there has been no progress toward promoting women to the top editorial positions since the day in 1977 when The Times itself said in an editorial, "As the lists of our company officers testify each day on this page, we are an institution run mostly by white men... Faced with social and legal pressures that we ourselves helped to generate, we have undertaken corrective measures, affirmative action, to expand opportunity in our company, in our profession and in our country."

The Times is no better and no worse than the national average. "Of the total 3,281 policy making positions listed in the 1982 E&P (Editor & Publisher) Yearbook, men occupy 2,966 and women 315 (representing a 90.4 percent share for men and 9.6 percent for women)," wrote Dorothy Jurney in the November 1982 Bulletin of the American Society of Newspaper Editors.

That's the reason why this and other discrimination suits against newspapers, television channels and news services are important to all women.

The Times suit is also an example of sex discrimination suits anywhere and in any industry. Note the typical progression of events:

• The suit was brought in 1974.
• Four years passed before it was settled.
• It was settled out of court as it became obvious that it would soon go to court with more than a good chance of being lost by the company (the women weren't backing down and the facts were there).
• Back pay was won.
• Affirmative action promises were made, with specific goals.
• The promises were only partly kept.
• The company claims to have met the requirements of the suit, but its own court-ordered statistical reports show that while it has more than met the goals in many categories, it has failed in others.
• The women will have to use every possible means to press for complete fulfillment of the promises, as more years drag by.

The New York Times Women's Caucus is now run by what one of the original plaintiffs calls "the second generation"—younger, newer women employees groomed by the old-timers to carry on the struggle.

Perhaps the most important lesson The Times suit can teach us is that we may win a battle but the war is unending.

The price of equality is eternal insistence.

For updates on The New York Times and other media employers: Media Report to Women, published by Women's Institute for Freedom of the Press, 3306 Ross Place, NW, Washington, DC 20008. Subscription is $20/year ($15 for individual women paying by personal check). Dorothy Jurney's statistics, quoted above, were reported in the January-February issue.

For 1980 statistics on female/male employment ratios in daily and Sunday newspapers, broadcasting and film direction, plus news about eight media suits, see "Media still in control of white males," EQUAL PAY, May/June 1981 issue.

© Copyright 1983 Paula Kassell

Names will never hurt us?

If language is a "trivial issue" why is our opposition so careful to use language that puts us on the defensive? And why do we fall into the trap of using words that hurt us?

There's a new phrase on this list, widely used (even by feminists)—the feminization of poverty, whose literal meaning is making poverty appropriate for women. The term that would express what has been happening to women and our rage about the shredding of the "safety net" is the pauperization of women, the term we should be using.

The earliest term on the list of words that hurt was bra burner, soon followed by women's libber. Neither name was of our choosing. Both were pasted on us by the media. But at least these epithets were never taken up and used by women who were feminists.

Not so for other hurtful phrases that we have sometimes been trapped into using ourselves:

• **pro-abortion** with its connotation of being in favor of women having abortions. What we are in favor of is the right of any woman to decide to undergo an abortion—we are pro-choice.

• **right-to-life**, one of the cleverest inventions of our opposition. We should be calling their philosophy compulsory pregnancy.

• **pro-family**, the term appropriated by the far right, is really pro-patriarchy in its most virulent form. Phyllis Schlafly, for example, calls herself pro-family and speaks out against battered women's shelters, because they interfere with marital relations.

• **working woman** exclusively for the woman who works for wages outside the home or the woman in the paid labor force, implying that the woman working at home caring for her family is not a working woman. Every time we use the specific terms we make an important point. Every time we don't we reinforce the terms that hurt us: working woman versus housewife or homemaker. There's nothing wrong with BEING a homemaker, but calling ourselves homemakers fails to make our point that we are women working at home.

The National Council of Churches has just published a new translation of bible readings for public worship, rewritten to eliminate references to God as male. "The image of God as father has been used to support the excessive authority of earthly fathers in patriarchal social system," is the explanation. Called The Inclusive Language Lectionary, it was prepared by a committee of bible scholars and pastors from several denominations of the Council, an organization of 30 Protestant and Eastern Othodox groups. Some of the significant changes in language:

• God's only child instead of Son.
• Children of God your Mother and Father instead of Sons of your Father.
• Human One instead of Son of Man.
• Friends instead of brethren.
• Sovereign instead of Lord.

All the news on the language front is not good. The New York Times still insists on labeling every woman Miss or Mrs. even when she objects and prefers Ms. Chairman, spokesman and all the other man-ending terms are still prevalent. Sarcastic keepers of the status quo are still laughing off the issue by suggesting "personhole" for "manhole." (is that a hole in a man?) The two terms are equally ridiculous—what they try to describe is an "access hole."

Desexifying terms, particularly those ending in "man", actually improves the language: letter carrier is informative while mailman is not; presiding officer or coordinator express the incumbent's functions; chairman and chairwoman are inherently meaningless. That's why substituting a functional term or the suffix person is the way to go. Changing to male and female suffixes fails to make our point that the sex of the person doing the job is irrelevant.

Even President Reagan is trying to avoid sexist language—he "has banished the word mankind from his vocabulary...

EQUAL PAY ♀
For Men Only

PAULA KASSELL

In Chicago, the mayor, the president of the University of Chicago, the city editor of the Chicago Tribune and the former president of the Chicago Bar Association—all women—are barred from membership in four of that city's top private luncheon clubs.

A woman arriving at a private club to make a presentation at a corporate or organization meeting might well be:
- Turned away from the club's main entrance and sent to the side door.
- Told that women may not sit in the lobby and sent to wait in a niche by the "ladies" room.
- Escorted to a private dining room to eat lunch alone while the male participants go to the main dining room.
- Barred from leaving the meeting with the men via the club's main stairway and sent to an elevator at the rear of the building (and the side door).

This kind of exclusion and humiliation is still widely accepted when it is directed against women, though now almost unthinkable against men from racial, religious or ethnic minorities.

Discrimination against women by private clubs and by service clubs is also a significant barrier against getting ahead. This is true whether the Kiwanis or Rotary is excluding the woman small business owner, or the Jaycees is excluding the young corporate executive, or the prestigious Metropolitan Club in Washington is excluding women members of Congress, or the Fort Orange Club in Albany is excluding women lobbyists and legislative aides.

Those who man the barriers against women claim that the clubs are private, social, only for comraderie. But fellow-members are recommended for job openings over the lunch table, leadership ability demonstrated in the clubs' service projects leads to promotions, the club directories list the members' businesses because they are expected to purchase each other's goods and services. Where does that leave the young women in management? On the lower rungs of the ladder. Where does that leave the female insurance or real estate or travel agent and the thousands of other small-town businesswomen who are excluded from Rotary and Kiwanis? Cut off from prime prospects.

Nevertheless, they—and all of us—are subsidizing this discrimination: dues and payment for club services paid by companies are tax deductible as business expenses, and the clubs themselves are tax exempt.

The turmoil within the Jaycees because of its men-only policy is a particular case in point. Scores of chapters have been trying to change it since the early '70s, encountering adamant refusal. Several court cases have resulted, brought by both sides—by the chapters against the organization, charging discrimination, and by the organization against the chapters for continuing to use the Jaycee name after admitting women.

The Jaycees' motto is "Build Tomorrow's Leaders Today." Its 64-year-old charter calls for admitting "young men" between the ages of 18 and 35. A woman can become a Jaycee-ette, but only if she is married to a Jaycee, and she is not even allowed to vote or hold office.

Jaycee chapters in cities in many parts of the country—Anchorage, Philadelphia, Newark, Memphis, Rochester, Boston, Chicago, Minneapolis and St. Paul and other places—have defied the state and national rules since 1972 by admitting women to full membership and electing them to office, even chapter president.

But national meetings, which are dominated, as is the organization, by small-town and rural chapters, voted in 1975, 1978 and 1981 to continue excluding women. The national executive board revoked the charters of chapters that did not oust their women members. Some chapters have just quit the Jaycees and continue as independent local groups.

So far, the courts have usually come down on the side of discrimination, starting with a federal ruling in 1972 that the Jaycees is a private organization not subject to the antidiscriminatory provisions of the Public Accommodation Law, even though the Jaycees receive millions of dollar in federal funds for their programs.

A notable exception are the Minnesota courts. First, in 1978 the Minneapolis and St. Paul chapters charged the organization with sex discrimination when the US Jaycees threatened to revoke their charter for admitting women. The State Human Rights Commission found that the Jaycees were a public accommodation under state law and that their leadership programs were, in effect, services sold in return for dues. The Minnesota Supreme Court upheld that finding in May 1981, and the federal district court agreed in March 1982. But in June 1983 the United States Court of Appeals for the Eighth Circuit reversed the lower court, holding that the sex discriminatory membership policies of the Jaycees were shielded by the organization's constitutional rights of association.

In January 1984, the US Supreme Court accepted an appeal filed by the state of Minnesota and agreed to decide whether private memberhip groups that deal with the public have a constitutional right to discriminate on the basis of sex in their choice of members.

WELCOME TO THE CLUB (no women need apply) by Lynn Hecht Shafran (Woman and Foundations/Corporate Philanthropy, 70 West 40 St., New York, NY 10018; (212) 997-1077) $3. My opening examples are from this booklet.

© 1984 Paula Kassell

Jaycees Finally Let Us In

The US Jaycees voted on August 16 to admit women to full membership. The vote was 5,372 to 386 with 77 abstentions, at a closed special meeting of national delegates in Tulsa. The men finally gave in after 12 years of resistance and legal fights that have cost the Jaycees $1 million.

It was new legal pressure that forced the change. The US Supreme Court ruled in July on a case brought by the State of Minnesota that states could compel the Jaycees to admit women under state law against discrimination. The laws of 37 states have public accommodations clauses that would apply to the Jaycees.

(Information from The New York Times)

See EQUAL PAY, March/April 1984 for the history of Jaycee resistance and background on the Minnesota case. See EQUAL PAY, May/June 1984 for insight into why men exclude women.

© Copyright 1984 Paula Kassell

EQUAL PAY

Recipe

1 cup crushed ego
1 teaspoon job discrimination
¼ teaspoon chauvinism
1 well-beaten path to the washing machine
½ teaspoon grated nerves
1 pinch from a man on the street
1 dash from the dentist to the babysitter

Mix all ingredients, one on top of the other, and stir violently. Cook until you feel a slow burn and add one last straw.

Serves: 53 percent of the population

Brenda Turner
1972

What's a Wife Worth?

PAULA KASSELL

What Is a Wife Worth? is the title of a new book by a Chicago matrimonial lawyer. Representing homemakers, he has succeeded in winning high divorce settlements after showing the court how much money a wife's services are worth—particularly in forwarding her husband's career at the expense of her own. But, as he rightly points out, wives in ongoing marriages—and their husbands—should also know her value.

What is a wife really worth? More than $40,000 a year if she is caring for two preschool children, this attorney, Michael Minton, says. He estimated the time spent on 23 chores by the average homemaker and then calculated how much it would cost a husband if he had to hire someone (more likely a crew) to do the work.

Mother of Two Preschool Children

job performed	Hours/week	Rate/hour	Value/week
Buyer, food & household goods	6	$ 5.75	$ 34.50
Nurse	11	5.14	56.54
Tutor	5	5.00	25.00
Waitress	21	3.41	71.61
Seamstress	1	3.20	3.20
Laundress	14	2.80	39.20
Chauffeur	0	5.50	—
Gardener	3.5	5.00	17.50
Family counselor	2.3	25.00	57.50
Maintenance worker	0	4.90	—
General Child Care	full time	174/week	174.00
Housekeeper	28	4.75	133.00
Cook	24	4.75	114.00
Maid	0	4.75	—
Interior decorator	.5	25.00	12.50
Dishwasher	14	4.00	56.00
Dietitian	12	5.00	60.00
Bookkeeper (home accounts)	0	4.35	—
		Weekly value	$ 854.55
		Yearly value (×52)	$44,436.50

Any homemaker could probably list 23 more chores that crop up. Note how low the hourly rates are and imagine what they should be if domestic work commanded wages comparable to what men earn for work like carpentry or housepainting. Even at these low rates, Minton points out that unpaid labor in the home is worth more than a secretary, for example, would be paid in the office.

It is possible, he goes on, for the replacement value of a homemaker to exceed the husband's earnings: "In fact, that is the whole idea."

New Directions for Women has been collecting and publishing these "what is a housewife worth?" computations for many years. In 1972 the Social Security Administration set it at $4,705 a year while two researchers at Cornell University pegged it at $10,000. By 1979 an expert on the Phil Donahue televsion show put it at $35,000 ("AUDIENCE: applause" says the transcript).

The total value of homemaking services in the United States was well over $350 billion (yes, BILLION) in 1974, according to the Clearinghouse on Women's Issues—one fourth of the nation's gross national product. But, of course, this work is never included in the GNP because it is based entirely on labor and production paid in dollars.

Why are these theoretical computations important? Because no woman who knows she is worth $44,436.50 a year will ever say—or think—"I'm just a housewife."

Further reading:

WHAT IS A WIFE WORTH? by Michael Minton with Jean Libman (William Morrow, 1983).

WOMAN'S WORK: The Housewife, Past and Present by Ann Oakley (Pantheon, 1974).

©1984 **Paula Kassell**

Affirmative Inaction

"Quotas" is the buzzword, but affirmative action is the victim. Actually, only four percent of affirmative action court cases are quota cases, according to Mary Frances Berry, a member of the US Commission on Civil Rights.

Saying that affirmative action goals and time tables mean abandoning the merit system, and using the slogan "reverse discrimination," the Reagan administration has scuttled enforcement of the Civil Rights Act of 1964 and many of the regulations that implemented it. Here are a few of its anti-enforcement actions:

• Budget cuts, of course. The Equal Employment Opportunity Commission, the federal enforcement agency, estimates it will process 8,000 fewer discrimination complaints in 1984 because of reduced operating funds.

• New regulations that exempt federal contractors with fewer than 250 employees and a contract under $1 million from written affirmative action programs. (The Secretary of Labor himself said this will free almost 75 percent of employers from this requirement.) The new rules also eliminate prior review of an employer's hiring patterns before awarding a federal contract. (Postponed indefinitely because of intense opposition from women's and civil rights groups.)

• A reconstituted Commission on Civil Rights with new Reagan appointees and a new executive director who proposed, among other changes, emphasizing possible adverse affects of affirmative action and racial quotas. The chair of the commission, a Reagan appointee, has said that "affirmative action discriminates against white men."

• Attempts to prevent or overturn agreements to promote minority public employees. The Justice Department went into court to try to overturn an agreement by the city of New Orleans to promote one Black police officer for every white officer until Blacks filled half the supervisory jobs. The Justice Department also opposed similar plans for the Detroit police and the Alabama highway patrol and intervened on the side of predominantly white police and firefighter unions, supporting seniority rights over recently hired Blacks in Cincinnati and Boston.

• The attempt to grant tax exemption to racist schools (the Bob Jones University case).

• A brief in support of exempting Grove City College from the laws against sex discrimination because, although students receive federal scholarship aid, the college itself takes no direct federal funds.

• And, the recent recommendation of a Justice Department official that the administration challenge a court ruling favorable to comparable worth in the State of Washington. The federal judge ordered back pay and wage increases totaling $800 million to $1 billion for some state employees. The wage increases will average 32 percent in female-dominated job categories, based on the state's own wage surveys and job evaluations. (Seventy-one members of Congress have signed a letter to the President taking issue with the recommendation and urging him to support the decision.)

BUT, ANOTHER KIND OF AFFIRMATIVE ACTION is all too evident in the Reagan administration—appointments for the president's cronies and campaign workers. Here are a couple of typical, little-noted examples to add to Reagan's disastrous appointments of his dear buddies that did make the prime-time news, and the special affirmative action Edward Meese exercised for his personal financial supporters:

• Robert Monks, former head of the Maine Republican Party and a substantial contributor to Vice President Bush's 1980 campaign, was named administrator of the Labor Department's pension welfare benefits system. He has some background in trust work, but his major involvement has been in coal and oil refineries.

• Donna Tuttle, daughter-in-law of one of the president's "kitchen cabinet" friends who advised him and raised money for his campaigns since he was governor of California, was appointed Under Secretary of Travel and Tourism in the Department of Commerce. Her resume showed no professional background in tourism, but she herself was active in Republican political campaigns.

THESE CHOICES WERE MADE BY THE MAN WHO, IF RE-ELECTED TO THE PRESIDENCY, WILL LIKELY APPOINT FOUR OR FIVE NEW SUPREME COURT JUSTICES, GIVEN THE AGE AND HEALTH OF SEVERAL CURRENT MEMBERS.

PAULA KASSELL

EQUAL PAY

PAULA KASSELL

When the subject is women and work, no matter where you start, you end up talking about sex segregation of jobs.

That was the case on June 5 when the Congressional Caucus for Women's Issues held a symposium on Low-Wage Work: Its Causes and Consequences. The meeting, in the Senate Office Building, was sponsored by the Women's Research & Education Institute (WREI), the nonpartisan research arm of the caucus.

This is what we heard:

• For 33 million Americans, nine out of ten of their coworkers are the same sex, Barbara Reskin pointed out.

• For example, in 300 large California firms employing 60,000 workers, fewer than one in ten employees share the same job title with the opposite sex, and even those are often segregated into different shifts or locations.

• Black women are more segregated into fewer industries than white women or black or white men. Over 70 percent are in the non-profit sector such as hospitals, Betty Wody told us.

• Black women over age 45 are even worse off. Lois Shaw explained that many older black women grew up in the south before the Supreme Court decision against segregated schools. Those few who went to college were persuaded to take home economics and nursing, where their classmates were almost certainly 100 percent female.

• About 35 percent of the earnings gap (with women's pay still hovering around 60 cents to men's dollar) is attributed to job segregation.

All this being so, is any progress being made to lessen the sex segregation of work? During the 1970s, 57 percent of the new workers entering the labor force were women. Did these 10 million women follow their sisters into women's work or push into men's jobs? Nancy Rytina and Suzanna Bianchi of the US Bureau of Labor Statistics have compared 1970 and 1980 census figures and found that, on the whole, not much changed.

The most significant movement in the distribution of the sexes was the increase in the number of women in a few managerial jobs—from 18 percent of the total in 1970 to 31 percent in 1980. But that is an exception. The proportion of women in most male occupations (defined as at least 80 percent male) did not change during the decade. Nor were men more apt to be in female occupations.

"Natural forces will not lead to job desegregation," said Barbara Reskin at the WREI symposium. Federal legislation has helped—industries targeted for enforcement show less segregation. The Vocational Education Act reauthorization bill currently before the Senate could make a difference to women in low-wage work. **Update**, the newsletter of the Congressional Caucus for Women's Issues, reported on May 31 that the Senate Labor and Human Resources Committee included a new provision requiring the states to spend vocational education funds on sex equity. The present bill only encourages the states to do so and they rarely appropriate the money for it. The result, documented at Congressional hearings during the past two years, is that our vocational education system remains sex-segregated and tends to train women and girls for low-paying, dead-end jobs.

But there are risks to desegregation, too. It has already happened that, as an occupation tips beyond integrations into a woman's job instead of a man's job—bank teller, insurance adjuster—the work is computerized, speeded up and closely monitored.

Does this mean that we can't win, no matter what we do? Of course not. What it indicates is that we are in a time of profound change with inevitable short-run dislocations. The profound change will be accomplished when we have achieved pay equity—when the wages of women and men are determined by the worth of their jobs, not by the sex of the job-holders.

Ronnie Steinberg brought to the symposium the good news that, both in the State of Washington and in Minnesota, if all the adjustments to bring women's pay into line with men's were made in one year, it would amount to about 4 percent of the personnel budget. So much for the predictions of those who warn that comparable worth wage-setting will upset the nation's entire economy.

Will men want to work at traditional women's jobs when they will pay as well as traditional men's jobs requiring comparable skills, effort and responsibility? That's unpredictable. Not in our lifetime, I bet. That's why "Separate But Equivalent: Perspectives on Comparable Worth" was the title of Ronnie Steinberg's subject at the Symposium on Low-Wage Work. Comparable worth policy has evolved to compensate for job segregation.

When the subject is women and work, no matter where you start, you end up talking about the sex-segregation of jobs.

When the subject is the sex-segregation of jobs, no matter where you start, you end up talking about comparable worth.

References

The Women's Research & Education Institute of the Congressional Caucus for Women's Issues, 204 Fourth St., SE, Washington, DC 20003 (202) 546-1090.

The Congressional Caucus for Women's Issues, 2471 Rayburn House Office Building, Washington, DC 20515 (202) 225-6740.

Barbara Reskin is Professor of Sociology and Women's Studies, Department of Sociology, University of Michigan. Bette Woody is Research Associate, Wellesley College Center for Research on Women. Lois Shaw is Research Scientist, Center for Human Resource Research, Ohio State University, Ronnie Steinberg is Director, Program in Comparable Worth, Center for Women in Government, State University of New York at Albany.

"Occupational Reclassification and Changes in Distribution by Gender," by Nancy F. Rytina and Suzannd M. Bianchi. Monthly Labor Review, March 1984.

©Copyright 1984 Paula Kassell

EQUAL PAY ♀

PAULA KASSELL

In Japan, female workers are exploited probably more than in any other industrialized country. So, as American business men eye the Japanese system that competes so successfully on the American market, do they give a thought to what happens to Japanese women?

The Japanese model is lifetime employment by one firm, starting immediately after graduation from college and lasting until retirement about 33 years later. What is usually left out of the story is that the model applies only to men. For women, employment traditionally lasts only until the birth of the first child. Most Japanese women are never given the opportunity to progress to more responsible, higher-paid positions. They fill staff, clerical, secretarial and technical assistant positions—and are required to serve tea to the men.

A graduate of prestigious Tokyo University, an office worker at Nissan Motor Company, said: "And the first thing a new woman has to learn is which cup belongs to whom." When she isn't serving tea, her work is much the same as the men her age. Most companies do not want to hire graduates of four-year colleges—junior college and high-school graduates are better suited to the job of "office lady." The companies also get a few more years of service by hiring the women younger.

Because most Japanese companies believe that when a woman becomes a homemaker she automatically becomes a less efficient employee, she is expected to resign, especially when she becomes pregnant. A 1974 study by the Women's and Minor's Bureau of the Japanese Ministry of Labor found that about 74 percent of women took less than the legal maternity and menstrual leave and many pregnant women do not ask for lighter work (even at the risk of miscarriage) because they fear being asked to resign.

The loyalty and conscientiousness of Japanese employees is what intrigues American management. The men go to work early, stay late and go in on weekends. **Japanese men entitled to two-week vacations take off an average of eight days.** Companies expect their male employees to be looked after by their homebound wives so that the husbands can give this full-time or overtime dedication to work.

In Japan, "looking after" a husband has a special meaning. Here is a description in a just-published book, **Japanese Women:**

It is not just that the husband depends on the wife's cooking, laundering, housecleaning, and whatnot, but that he comes to rely on her service "around the body." In the morning he needs his wife's help in finding a complete set of clothing to wear that day. "Every morning, I put out one thing after another, saying, 'Here are your socks, here's your shirt, here's your handkerchief and so forth.' " The wife may help him put on a tie and coat, and place his shoes, which she has polished, where he can put them on easily.

The around the body care resumes upon the husband's return from work. . . The wife is called upon to help him change clothes, to serve him at table, and to bring him whatever he wants—cigarettes, an ashtray, a glass of water or a newspaper. When he relaxes to watch television, all he has to do is call out: "Channel eight!" whereupon she rushes in from the next room where she is working to turn the dial.

Obviously, embracing the Japanese system would set American corporations in direct opposition to the changes feminists have been advocating and young families have been adopting since the 1970s. Young fathers want more time and involvement with their children, not less. Young mothers want life-time careers, not temporary jobs.

The top American executives envying the Japanese model may already be living much like that workaholic rat-race. Do we want them to set the rest of us on the same course? Is the bottom line worth it?

References:

Working Women in Japan by Alice H. Cook and Hiroko Hayashi (Cornell University, New York State School of Industrial and Labor Relations) 1980.

"Japan's New Breed of 'Office Ladies' " by Steve Lohr. **The New York Times,** Dec. 27, 1983.

Japanese Women by Takie Sugiyama Lebra (University of Hawaii Press) 1984.

Ordeal By Press

"Is the press fair to Ferraro?" Newsweek asked that question and found innuendoes in lieu of facts in The Wall Street Journal, The Philadelphia Inquirer and New York Magazine. "The issue," Newsweek concluded, "is not what journalists decide to investigate, but what they decide to print."

And how about the grueling two-hour press conference after she released her own and her husband's financial figures? One reporter was so aggressively mean in his questioning that he was booed by the other journalists. But she defended herself with such skill and forcefulness that the reporters applauded her at the end of the conference. Have you ever heard of such happenings before?

At the same time the press was hassling Ferraro about entanglement in her husband's business affairs, they were giving her the same old sexist treatment—showing her shopping for groceries, describing her clothes and haircut. Even more important, her stand on abortion—in favor of freedom of choice—has been endlessly pursued. Mondale has the same stand on abortion, but the press has not focussed on that to the neglect of other issues. Reagan takes the opposite stand, but the mass media have done little to alert the public to the horrible potential effects of his policy.

Aside from the set-back Ferraro's ordeal-by-press could have dealt her candidacy and the Democratic campaign, there is a much larger issue here. Most married women who will run for offfice in the future will have husbands involved in a business or a profession, a government job or another political office. Will the husband's work and his other interests forever dominate and take precedence over a female candidate's own background and qualifications?

We are certainly not asking this question to promote equally fierce attacks on male candidates' wives, who up to now have been practically immune from scrutiny. That's not the kind of fair treatment we want to see.

The point is that the press has failed when we go into the voting booth knowing infinitely more about John Zaccaro's real estate deals than we do about Geraldine Ferraro's voting record in Congress and her stands on all issues.

PAULA KASSELL

Hot Conference Holds Promise

PAULA KASSELL

No one can predict whether the delegates at the third official United Nations Conference on Women in Nairobi, Kenya, will overcome the political issues dividing them and adopt the main conference document, "Forward Looking Strategies for the Year 2000 for the Advancement of Women." Two months prior to the opening date, the preparatory committee had not even agreed whether to adopt it by vote or by consensus, and 90 controversial paragraphs were yet to be resolved.

But Forum '85, the parallel meeting of women taking place in Nairobi at the same time, is expected to have an entirely different dynamic, a "good spirit," says Dame Nita Barrow, the convenor of the Forum planning committee. Forum '85, sponsored by the non-governmental organizatons (NGOs) with consultative status at the UN, is open to anyone who can get to Nairobi. By mid-May, 5,500 people from all over the world had already registered, and requests to give over 1,000 workshops had been submitted.

Forum '85 will run from July 10 to July 19 at Nairobi University. The official UN governmental conference is July 15-26, at Kenyatta Center. The Nairobi gatherings mark the end of the United Nations Decade for Women.

The first UN World Conference on Women in Mexico City in 1975 (International Women's Year) adopted a World Plan of Action setting minimum goals for the advancement of women in many areas, such as education, employment, political participation and policy-making and recognition of the economic value of women's work in the home. Themes of the decade have been Equality, Development and Peace.

In 1980, 145 nations gathered in Copenhagen for the Mid-Decade conference, with Employment, Health and Education added as sub-themes. A World Plan of Action was accepted.

The 1975 and 1980 governmental conferences were torn asunder by political conflicts and are remembered more for the "Zionism Is Racism" resolutions and the divisive incidents stressed by the media than for their statements on women's issues. Largely forgotten, for example, is the Convention on the Elimination of Discrimination Against Women signed in Copenhagen and since ratified by 66 nations, but not the US.

Each governmental conference had a simultaneous parallel conference open to the world public, called the Tribune in Mexico City and The Forum in Copenhagen. Thousands of women from many countries gathered to exchange ideas and experiences and to challenge the boundaries of their lives. The participants held hundreds of seminars, workshops and informal discussions—resulting in new perspectives, new networks, new organizations and new strategies for change.

One example of networking planned for the 1985 meetings is the Women's International News Service, which is sending a team of two dozen feminist journalists from the US to Nairobi to coordinate print, radio and television coverage of both the UN meeting and the Forum for US feminist and mass media. A home team (see box) will distribute daily teletype dispatches to the US mass media through a receiving center in Terre Haute, IN. The project is sponsored by the Women's Institute for Freedom of the Press with assistance from the Skaggs Foundation.

Some women at the Forum may be "torn between loyalty to feminism and loyalty to their oppressed groups," as one NGO representative put it. But Bella Abzug, who chairs the American Jewish Congress committee on Nairobi, believes women are much better prepared this time to put their differences aside and concentrate on the problems of women and children. Abzug told NEW DIRECTIONS FOR WOMEN that even Palestinian women she has talked to are saying, "The men are still carrying guns but they're not worrying about my equality."

Arvonne Fraser, who was in the US delegation to both previous US conferences, expects to see women at Forum 85 coalescing around areas of interest and expertise across national boundaries. Fraser is director of the Women, Public Policy and Development Project of the Hubert Humphrey Institute at the University of Minnesota.

"I think we will come out of Nairobi with a lot of new networks based on subject matter, including a lot of new international networks," Fraser predicted. "I keep saying there's a women's underground and the media can write about the politics and we'll foment the revolution—a very quiet revolution."

For more information:

Forum '85. For brochure, send self-addressed stamped envelope to Forum Planning Committee, 777 UN Plaza 11th floor, New York, NY 10017.

"How to Participate in the World Women's Conference Without Leaving Home." Send self-addressed stamped envelope to Women, Public Policy and Development Project, 909 Social Science Building, 267 19th Ave. South, University of Minnesota, Minneapolis, MN 55455.

Decade Update (bulletins). International Women's Tribune Centre, 777 UN Plaza, New York, NY 10017.

United Nations World Conference on Women. For brochure: Leticia Shahani, Secretary General, 1985 Women's Conference, Branch for the Advancement of Women. CSDHA, Vienna International Centre, PO Box 500, A-1400, Vienna, Austria.

Bitter class action suit against church

MERIKAY MCLEOD

BETRAYAL by Merikay McLeod (Mars Hill Publications, P.O. Box 362, Loma Linda, CA 92354)

PAULA KASSELL

Betrayal, Merikay McLeod Silver's true story, is an appalling but fascinating example of men of seemingly good will preying on the trust of a woman who had faith in their integrity. I stayed up most of a night reading the day-by-day story of the emotional battering of one young, believing, trusting woman by powerful—and sometimes personable—church leaders. Friends who helped and supported her were also under attack —sometimes subtle and sometimes blatant. The men failed to cow her, and in the end they failed to best her.

In 1971, Merikay Silver went to work as an editor for Pacific Press Publishing Association of the Seventh-Day Adventist Church. In 1972, finding out that she was making less than half of what a male editor was making, she asked for equal pay. The reason for her lower salary was that she did not have a college degree, but she was an experienced editor and had written best sellers for the press.

When she also discovered that male employees were given "head-of-household" benefits, she requested the same pay and benefits a married man in her position would receive. Her husband had lost his job and wanted to return to school for a degree. At the press, even married men with wives earning $800 a month (twice what Merikay was making) were receiving head-of-household salaries.

She was stunned to hear the press manager explain that giving her what she wanted would cause a problem with the women in the bindery. She realized that even those who were widows and divorcees raising children alone or supporting invalid husbands or parents were not getting the benefits either—that no woman in the entire institution received head-of-household pay. And through a secretary she learned that married men were given one dollar an hour rent allowances, single men 70 cents an hour and all women 30 cents an hour.

The church's own personnel guidelines required that basic salary scales and living allowances were to be paid "without discrimination on the basis of race, religion, sex, age, national origin or color." Nevertheless, what ensued was years of stalling, appeals to her loyalty to the church and the press, a long talk with a high church official she was certain she could trust (he later lied on the witness stand)—and finally a long court case.

Perhaps the book title should be "Betrayal and Loyalty", in recognition of Lorna Tobler, the secretary who risked her career and her husband's (both longtime employees of Pacific Press) to find in the company's records the evidence needed to prove discrimination. A few months after she started helping Silver, the press transferred her husband to Germany and repeatedly pressured Lorna to join him, even threatening that he might lose his job if she did not go. She refused to leave because Silver needed her. When the press fired Lorna in 1973, she filed retaliation charges.

On and on, back and forth, this painful case goes. Neither side would give up. Silver was loyal to the other women employees in the class action suit. The press and church officials could not bear to relinquish their managership-of-household traditions. (They're still at it. This spring the Seventh-Day Adventist Church refused to ordain a woman as a minister; she graduated at the top of her seminary class. Not only that—she had spent her own time and money, while men are subsidized to go through seminary.)

At the end of the book, Merikay writes of the Pacific Press trauma as the great divide of her life. "Before the Press I was someone else, living in a different world...I no longer belong to the church..." The tensions of the press struggle eventually destroyed her marriage. She tells of the separation and divorce from her husband, Kim Silver; then she resumed her birth name, Merikay McLeod.

I won't spoil the mystery of how it all turned out, but in 1977, Merikay's sixth-grade church-school teacher told her that after nearly 35 years of teaching within the denominational school system, she was finally receiving a pay increase that would raise her income to equal the men teachers'. A fitting outcome.

Merikay McLeod now runs her own media relations firm, Merik Communications, and produces a San Francisco Bay area public-service television program, Women Working.

New feminism examined

CONTROVERSY AND COALITION: The New Feminist Movement by Myra Marx Ferree and Beth B. Hess (Twayne Publishers) $17.95

PAULA KASSELL

This is a book I thought I could skim through in an hour. After all, I worked in the New Feminist Movement of the late 60s, 70s and 80s as an activist and was part of it as it was happening. I was wrong. I read every page to follow Beth Hess's and Myra Marx Ferree's analysis of the whats and whys. I found new insights. So, I predict, will other women activists.

Imagine, then, what is in store for women who were not so involved, and especially for young women of high school and college age who may be unaware of how their opportunities were made possible. They will never take their luck for granted again.

As the title **Controversy and Coalition** indicates, one core of the book describes and explains how conflicts developed. An important divisive issue today is the anti-Semitism expressed by Black women. The authors point out that Jewish women have been prominent in the feminist movement far beyond their proportion in the population, and in the civil rights movement as well. The implication is that anti-Semitism sometimes underlies the harsh criticisms that Black women level at feminists who plan meetings and events, no matter what the agenda or outreach efforts.

The authors, both sociology professors, have organized their book around different strands of feminism; they have described the development of the "bureaucratic" strand (commissions on women, organizations like NOW) and the "collectivist" strand (women who seceded from the New Left Movement to form feminist groups). One chapter traces the four basic routes feminists are traveling: (1) career feminism: desegregrating the labor force, (2) liberal feminism: working for equal rights under the law, (3) socialist feminism: challenging capitalism (rejecting a focus on individual advancement because it is society as a whole that needs to be emancipated) and (4) radical feminism: expanding visions of community (trying separatism to build a model in miniature of a world without patriarchy).

The other core is coalition. Fierce opposition to passage of the Equal Rights Amendment and continual attempts to undermine and restrict the right to legal abortion (both going on to this day) stimulated strong coalition to work for these feminist issues. Over 100 major organizations supported ratification of the ERA and more than 100,000 people marched on the Capitol in Washington to pressure Congress to extend the deadline for ratification. The ERA failed but the coalition is renewing the campaign for another try. Even more significant: a wide spectrum of women's groups, from old to new, from the traditional to the radical, are still pooling their resources and lobbying strength to work together on many feminist issues.

Posing the question "Will those who are now only children ever understand what feminism is all about?" Ferree and Hess answer with optimism. They cite Alice Rossi's two-step, two-generation process. The first generation (the old war horses like myself), angered by the limits imposed on women, struggles to achieve changes. The second generation lives the new lives and explores the opportunities created. The third generation, blithely expecting to "have it all," experiences the more subtle but equally effective remaining limits most acutely, and becomes again the first generation, struggling to remove these restraints. My granddaughter will grow up to be one of the strugglers, I hope.

The authors' final words: "And so feminism is, and will continue to be, reborn and redefined in every generation." So be it!

Speaking personally

PAULA KASSELL

Meeting in circles—visioning—freeing ourselves from internalized oppression—hearing into being—affirming ourselves and one another—the living newspaper—the chronicle. These are all part of the unusual, stunningly successful processes of Women Gathering dreamed up and planned by Sonia Johnson and her colleagues, Susan Horwitz and Mary Ann Beall. I was lucky; I took part in the first national Women Gathering, in Washington, August 1983. It was a unique weekend—not a conference, not a social event, not therapy—a joyful, warm, loving and sometimes painful experience that left me glowing physically and mentally.

So many women at that first gathering felt the same way that local or statewide gatherings have been set up all over the country since 1983, including a one-day New Jersey gathering later that year, which I also went to with great pleasure, though one day is really not enough time to fully savor the process. The second national Women's Gathering was in St. Louis, August 1984 (I missed that one).

But I have just returned, again feeling like a new woman, from the third national gathering, called by the New Jersey aficianadas, in Convent Station this August. I mean that literally: I pride myself on being realistic, yet my mind blossomed with visions; I am cool and reserved, slow to warm to people, and not expressive, yet the eight other women in my circle became my sisters overnight. We laughed and shed tears together and healed each others' hurts with hugs and concern.

The processes are devised to combine creative visioning with hard thinking about our ideal post-patriarchal future world. At the same time each woman in turn is focussing on a forceful affirmation for her own future, prodded and supported by the others in the circle.

Visioning starts with imagining sensory experiences—smelling, tasting, touching, seeing, feeling. Then comes visioning around the question: What kind of world do we want? In each circle of nine women a recorder makes two lists—the group's key images of what we don't want in our perfect future world (sexual division of labor, power struggles, high heels, conformity, original sin, national boundaries, refined foods, Falwell, etc., etc.) and what we do want (safe effective birth control, a world of non-violence and peace, the right to revel in our own sexuality and creativity, comfortable clothing with pockets, teaching of feminist principles, equal pay for comparable worth, etc. etc.). Every circle's list is posted on the wall for all to share. By the end of the weekend, the gym walls are papered with the living newspaper, the lists made during all the processes, later published as the chronicle of the gathering and sent to the participants.

Hearing Into Being, the second process, takes place in groups of three. Each woman talks uninterrupted for one-half hour (or she can remain silent for part of her time) while the other two listen intently but without showing any reaction whatsoever. There are two sessions on different days. Three basic questions are addressed: What kind of world do we want? What has to change to bring it about? How do we make these changes? Returning to the full circle of nine women, the ideas are shared, recorded and hung on the wall.

Affirmation is the tough part of the process. Gathered in the circle of nine, each woman is asked five questions: (1) What do you love about women? (2) What do you dislike about the way women behave because of our conditioning? (3) When have you stood up against the oppression of women? (4) When have you cooperated in the oppression of women? (5) What is it about yourself that you'd like to believe but find most difficult? (What wonderful thing do you find hardest to believe about yourself? What do your friends say about you that you'd love to believe but you can't?)

If a woman needs help with question five, in phrasing and declaiming an affirmation that bares her soul (and many do), the deep trust and empathy already built up within the group give her courage. (I am a completely lovable woman just as I am, I am an excellent public speaker, I am a superb organizer, my vulnerability is my greatest strength, I am free to let go, I don't care what people think, I am a totally attractive person, I love myself, I am a winner, etc. etc.).

The work in the circles is of course the core of the process, but there are also the good times when all the circles (about 150 women) come together—singing, visioning, doing exercises, listening. Especially listening to Sonia Johnson, our charismatic Sonia, whose keynote speech is the highlight of every gathering. The ideas she brings are as far-out as the processes.

As I drove home from my first gathering, I was reminded of the early days of the feminist movement when consciousness-raising was making sisters of us all. It was a long time ago, and it is a long time since I received a letter signed "in sisterhood." But the Women Gatherings are a strong revival: Sisterhood Is Still Powerful.

The August 1986 Women Gathering will be in the Pittsburgh area. For information: Linda Morrow, 140 Walnut St., Beaver, PA 15009; (412) 774-6045. I'll be there.

Facts Debunk Sociobiology

MYTHS OF GENDER: Biological Theories About Women and Men by Anne Fausto-Sterling (Basic Books) $18.95

PAULA KASSELL

In 1980 Camilla Benbow and Julian Stanley wrote a short research article in **Science** magazine claiming statistical evidence that boys are innately better at math than girls. The media jumped at it—**Time** and **Newsweek** even used radio ads hawking the new evidence about "male math genes" in their latest issues. Newspapers, radio stations and TV channels around the country made sure that scarcely a child or adult would remain ignorant of this latest "proof" of female inferiority.

Scientists have been coming up with these "biology is destiny" messages for thousands of years. Somehow biology always destines males for genius, achievement and leadership and females for lagging behind. Every claim has been dishonored. Yet the vision of proof that women are inferior seems to be irresistible.

"Early studies, which discovered that male brains were larger than female brains, concluded that the female's smaller size resulted in her inferior intelligence." This logic, Anne Fausto-Sterling points out, "runs afoul of the 'elephant problem': if size were the determinant of intelligence, then elephants and whales ought to be in command."

One of the latest attempts focuses on left-right hemisphere specialization—female brains are said to be less specialized, and this interferes with our ability to perform spatial tasks (in engineering and architecture, for example). There is even a theory that geniuses are usually male because of the way they inherit the X-chromosome (part of the theory is that a number of genes relating to intellectual ability reside on it).

"And the idea that women's reproductive systems direct their lives is ancient," Anne Fausto-Sterling reminds us in her chapter on menstruation, menopause and female behavior. "But whether it was Plato, writing about the disruption caused by barren uteri wandering about the body, Pliny, writing that a look from a menstruating woman will 'dim the brightness of mirrors, blunt the edge of steel and take away the polish from ivory,' or modern scientists writing about the changing levels of estrogen and progesterone, certain messages emerge quite clearly. Women, by nature emotionally erratic, cannot be trusted in positions of responsibility."

Myths of Gender has finally come along to discredit the modern purveyor of such nonsense: sociobiology, the systematic study of the biological basis of all social behavior. Among its purposes: to reform anthropology, psychology and sociology by "biologicizing them."

Randy Thornhill, for instance, describes insect and animal behavior as rape after studying scorpionflies, bedbugs, ducks and monkeys. Thus, rape becomes, to him, a natural phenomenon. Thornhill goes on to apply his observations of insects to humans, leading ultimately to the attitude that men raping women is excusable.

The beauty of **Myths of Gender** is that Fausto-Sterling picks apart this and other sociobiologists' experiments and observations. She shows how they were flawed or that the conclusions did not really follow from the results. And she does it with wit, humor and some well deserved sarcasm. This is not a difficult book, luckily, because it is an important one.

Fausto-Sterling takes on all the controversial biological theories—about intelligence, genius, menstruation, menopause, female athletic ability, male aggression, evolution. Each analysis is so detailed that excerpting is impossible. But reading **Myths of Gender** is balm to our undermined female egos. The title tells all. Having been battered for centuries with pronouncements and "scientific" proof that we are inferior to males in almost every way, we need the ammunition that this valuable book gives us.

Feminist Career Photographs

1. Working as editor and publisher of the new feminist periodical *New Directions for Women in New Jersey* (Dover, NJ, 1972)

2. Publicity shot (1975)

3. Still working on *New Directions for Women*, now a national periodical (Dover, NJ, 1990)

4. Featured in the Morris County Historical Society exhibit on New Jersey Feminists (Morristown, NJ, 2000–2001)

Miss. . Mrs. . Mrs. . Ms.

PAULA KASSELL

This is about the power of one man—A.M. Rosenthal, executive editor of The New York Times, who refused for 15 years to add "Ms.," to the paper's stylebook, and the power of one woman—me. It's the true story of how it came to pass that on June 20, 1986, The New York Times announced, "Beginning today, The New York Times will use 'Ms.' as an honorific in its news and editorial columns..."

The tale starts back in the early '70s with letters-to-the-editor from many women, including myself (a few were published, mine were not). The Times offices were even picketed in 1974 by Times women and other feminists. Over the years the letters kept coming and Rosenthal was cornered at dinner parties and other gatherings, to no avail. "I'm too macho to give in to the women," he told me on one of those occasions.

Unlike Abe Rosenthal, other Times people allowed their dislike of the term to give way to need. William Safire wrote in The New York Times Magazine of August 5, 1984: "It breaks my heart to suggest this, but the time has come for Ms. We are no longer faced with a theory, but a condition. It is unacceptable for journalists to dictate to a candidate that she call herself Miss (Ferraro) or else use her married name... Ms. is deliberately mysterious, but at least it is not misleading." A note "From the Editors" following Safire's piece said, among other inanities, "As for Ms.,—that useful businessletter coinage—we reconsider it from time to time; to our ear, it still sounds too contrived for news writing." The brain might have produced a more intelligent evaluation.)

Abe Rosenthal obviously paid no attention to the letters-to-the editor about the real problems of inaccuracy and inconsistency caused by shunning "Ms." Casey Miller and Kate Swift, authors of Words and Women, had written in a letter published in 1974, deploring The Times unwillingness to adopt "Ms.": "For the few women who feel the need to be identified by their particular circumstance of having or not having a spouse (dead or alive, divorced or separated or never existed, as well as present and accounted for), there is a simple solution The Times might adopt: courtesy is more important than consistency."

Diane Reis of the New York State Division of Human Rights pointed out in a 1982 letter that the New York State Human Rights Law was amended in 1975 to include marital status as a protected classification. "Therefore," she went on, "if it is illegal in New York State for an employer, rental agent, bank officer, etc., to inquire into a person's marital status, how can the specification of one's marital status be considered an acceptable written practice?"

All the letters, all the petitions by Times reporters and editors for reconsideration were brushed aside. So in the pages of The Times every woman was referred to as "Miss" or "Mrs." whether she liked it or not and by guesswork when she refused to tell the reporter her marital status, incensed, as many newsworthy women were, by this outdated labeling by relationship to a man.

What provoked the about face? This dialogue between me and Arthur Ochs Sulzberger, the publisher, on April 30 at The Times annual stockholders meeting (I bought the stock for just such a purpose):

PK: I am Paula Kassell. You may recall that I have raised issues of interest to feminists at previous meetings.

AOS: Nods "yes."

PK: I want to commend you for the substantive response you made to an issue I have raised in the past. (I objected to The Times paying for dues and services at clubs that did not admit women members. The practice was stopped shortly thereafter.)

AOS: Nods "yes."

PK: Now I want to bring up the subject of the non-use of the honorific "Ms." by The Times. I know that publishers take pride in not interfering with editorial decisions. But you as publisher and I as a stockholder have a right to expect that editorial decisions be made on a rational basis. I request that the decision not to use "Ms." in the pages of The Times be subjected to rational discussion.

Daily inaccuracies occur, caused solely by restricting women's honorifics to "Miss" and "Mrs." I have been referred to as Miss Kassell in the pages of The Times and as Mrs. Kassell, and all the time my marital status had not changed.

Your daughter Karen retained her name when she married. Did she become Mrs. Sulzberger?

AOS: I've been trying to figure that out myself.

PK: In half to three quarters of the wedding reports in The New York Times on a Sunday, the bride is reported to be retaining her name. More and more women are retaining their names. Every one is a potential problem to The Times reporters, editors and proofreaders as these women do newsworthy things.

AOS: One of our editors brought it up to me a few months ago that he thought it was time for us to reconsider the use of "Ms."

PK: The Times has changed its policy on the use of honorifics in the past. As you know, The Times would not use "Mr." before the names of criminals or unsavory characters. This policy was changed in 1973.

Now I challenge the publisher of The Times to challenge the editors to debate the pros and cons of the use of "Ms." with consultants on language usage. Members of The Times Women's Caucus are well prepared to take the pro side, and I recommend Alma Graham of McGraw-Hill as an authority on non-sexist language. The editors can bring to the debate all their reasons for not using "Ms." You should be very interested in seeing that list. I know I would be. I predict it could be written on a very small piece of paper.

AOS: I will accept your challenge.

Two weeks later came a letter from the publisher, worth quoting in full:

Dear Ms. Kassell:

You see what you have done to me? (I guess I made him call me "Ms.")

As I said I would, I have discussed this matter with our executive editor. He, in turn, is discussing it with some of his colleagues and will get back to me. I am not sure we need to go outside our own institution for help.

In any event, I am sharing your letter with Mr. Rosenthal in case he wishes to follow your suggestion. (I had sent the publisher Alma Graham's address after the stockholders meeting.)

Thanks for your interest.

Sincerely,
(signed) Arthur
Ochs Sulzberger

A month later came another letter from the publisher:

Dear Ms. Kassell:

Midst great cheers from the women (and many of the men) who serve as reporters and editors of The New York Times, the attached notice was posted on the bulletin board.

Thank you for raising the issue at the Annual Meeting.

Sincerely,
(signed) Arthur
Ochs Sulzberger

Here is the full text of the notice:

Memorandum for the staff from A.M. Rosenthal—

EDITOR'S NOTE: Beginning today, The New York Times will use "Ms." as an honorific in its news columns.

Until now, "Ms.," had not been used because of the belief that it had not passed sufficiently into the language to be accepted as common usage.

The Times believes now that "Ms." has become a part of the language, and is changing its policy.

The Times will continue to use "Miss," or "Mrs." when it knows the marital status of a woman in the news unless she prefers "Ms."

"Ms." will also be used when a woman's marital status is not known, or when a married woman wishes to use her maiden name professionally or in private life.

(signed) AMR
June 19, 1986

I haven't figured out what to bring up at the next stockholders meeting. Any ideas?

1986 - Year of Red Herrings

My passions have been aroused by the mass media's unrelenting campaign to make Americans believe that the feminist movement is "in disarray," "has peaked" and that "women" (implying we are all alike) regret not being full-time housewives and mothers.

No! This is a time to exult. If the feminist movement were really self-destructing, the opposition would not be acting like dinosaurs facing extinction from a radically changed environment. Polls show that more women—and men—prefer today's roles for themselves and each other.

But the mass media worked hard in 1986 to convince us otherwise. Three attacks stand out for wide coverage from prestigious newspapers and magazines, hometown weeklies and, of course, television and radio.

Old Maids at 30

One popular story tells us that if we are not married by 30, our statistical chances of getting a husband are slim, and growing slimmer with advancing age. Based on research unpublished because the researchers were not satisfied with it, here is how the media's figures compare with the U.S. Census Bureau's, which were collected by accepted statistical methods, as the unpublished studies were not:

College-educated women at 30 have a 20 percent chance at marriage, say the stories in the media; the Census Bureau pegs their chances at 66 percent. Women at 40 have a 2.6 percent chance, say the media; a 23 percent chance says the Census Bureau.

And so what, anyway? Obviously many women enjoy the delicious independence of living alone, others prefer living with women, and more and more are living with men without tying themselves up in marriage.

Back to "the feminist mystique"?

The second media blitz is about the professional women—lawyers and doctors are usually used as examples—and the successful women in management who are opting out. Tired of the superwoman role, goes the story, they are quitting their jobs to stay home, perhaps with young children or to have a first baby "before it is too late." The stories imply they will be home, not for weeks or months, but for years—maybe forever. And the articles are written to imply that this is a flood, not a trickle.

I don't believe it. Women have always moved in and out of jobs to accommodate family. For every woman leaving there are others ready to come back. But the stories are not written to show that. What makes me maddest—and saddest—is that so many women in the media have fallen for it, accepted assignments to write about it and churned out superficial, one-sided human-interest pieces about a few attorneys or corporate hot-shots (never media women) who have opted out. They have not given us the balanced view we have a right to expect from journalists who, for the most part, consider themselves (and I agree) feminists or at least in tune with feminist aims.

I was disappointed (but not surprised) that the American newswomen at the big International Women's Media Conference in November focused almost entirely on their problems of getting to the top, leaving it mostly to the delegates from other countries to bring up the problems of covering women's news. Only Marvine Howe of The New York Times stood up to remind the American women that "we have everything to thank the women's movement for. My personal choice was to be a foreign correspondent but I don't think I'd be here today if it weren't for the women's movement."

Blaming Feminists Again

The third media attack was a gleeful dance around a book that puts the blame for women's problems (see above) on the feminist movement and NOW (often seen as synonymous). I suspect that's why the book, Sylvia Ann Hewlett's *A Lesser Life: The Myth of Women's Liberation in America*, was given so much press and TV publicity. Hewlett holds NOW and the movement responsible for our having no maternity and parental leave law as European countries do, claims feminists have paid only lip service to child care, and criticizes the Equal Rights Amendment. There is no point in outlining or reviewing the book here (see the May/June 1986 issue). The point is the way the media turned somersaults over it.

We Won't Swallow These Red Herrings

These red herrings don't convince me. We who read feminist newspapers know about the current ferment of blue collar, Black and Latina women organizing on the grassroots level, sometimes funded by wealthy women—a new wrinkle. We remember the Forum of the World Conference of Women in Nairobi in 1985.

The men who own and manage most of the mass media newspapers, magazines and broadcast stations and channels have a perfect right to feed us whatever they wish—that's what ownership buys. And that's why for 15 years we have devoted our days and nights and minds and hearts and resources to owning and managing **New Directions for Women**, so we can bring you the truth. For 15 years we have uncovered and published the untold news about the lives of women—battered women, incest, displaced homemakers, poverty—years before the mass media caught up.

You've never been served a red herring from our hands!

PAULA KASSELL

Some newspapers and magazines have given space to counteracting articles—for example, Katha Pollitt in The Nation, Ellen Goodman in her syndicated column, Susan Faludi in West Magazine, Jennifer Chrichton in Ms. For information about these and other debunking pieces, contact News About Women, NOW Legal Defense and Education Fund, 1776 K St., NW, #900, Washington, DC 20006; (202) 429-7339. For Catherine East's "Critical Comments on A Lesser Life" send $5 to National Women's Political Caucus, 1275 K St., NW, Suite 750, Washington, DC 20005; (202) 898-1100.

Clothes Make The Woman...

PAULA KASSELL

For centuries clothes have made clear what each culture expects its males and females to look like. That's the point of a fascinating show at the Smithsonian National Museum of American History in Washington, DC (through May 1991). The show is titled Men and Women: A History of Costume, Gender and Power.

The viewer moves through corridor after corridor lined on one side with cases of female clothes, cosmetics and accessories, and male outer garments, underwear and paraphenalia on the other. It's quite amazing to see how the human body is made to change shape as the decades pass, switching from ideals of plumpness to slimness, from hourglass to rectangle and back again. How we have been manipulated in our slavery to fashion!

Even today, how few of us have rebelled. Short skirts and high heels make women look and feel weak and vulnerable. Jackets and tight collars make men hot and sweaty, and their styles are so limited that men look like carbon copies of each other.

Including men in a costume exhibit gives a whole new, consciousness-raising picture of fashion. Scepticism set in as I entered the exhibit and read that it was supported by a grant from the National Cosmetology Association. But this led to parallel displays in case after case of male as well as female cosmetics in addition to clothes from the 1700s to the present.

Men have been enhancing their aura with bay rum, brilliantine, scented shaving soaps and lotions during all these centuries. And their jewelry included not just necklaces, bracelets, pins and rings, but even earrings.

In the 1700's men wore ruffles, silver buckles, decorative garters, conspicuous colors and fancy silks and laces. By the 1840s all that had been abandoned by males and become identified as feminine.

Surprisingly, the hourglass figure fashionable in the 1840s—rounded shoulders and hips accentuated by a small waist—was prescribed for men as well as women. But for women the shape was created by tight, restricting corsets while padding built into men's clothes created a broad chest and shoulders and fullness below the waist.

The fitness craze of today is another parallel affecting both sexes but carried out in a way detrimental to women: the ideal for men is to develop muscular power and strength, but the ideal for women is a slim youthful figure, leading to obsession with dieting.

The display about the Miss America contests in Atlantic City was an unexpected bonus. The contests were started in 1921, abandoned from 1927 to 1935 because influential hotels complained that their patrons objected to the display of semi-nude female bodies. Then they were revived in 1937 and talent competitions were added.

The famous feminist picketing and demonstration on the boardwalk in Atlantic City during the 1968 contest has a display case of its own, with a trash can and the "symbols of oppression" that the demonstrators threw into it—bras, girdles, high-heeled pumps and big curlers. Bras were never burned, the exhibit script makes clear.

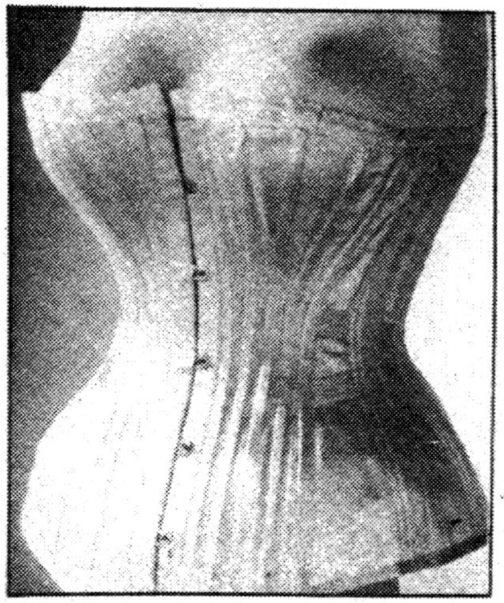

The show's curator, Barbara Clark Smith of the Costume Division of the museum, is evidently a true sister in feminism. Try to see her exhibit before it closes in May 1991. It's an eye-opener.

The Smithsonian has published a book based on the script of the exhibit: Men and Women: A History of Costume, Gender, and Power by Barbara Clark Smith and Kathy Price ($6.95).

The Smithsonian has also published a valuable related book: Men and Women: Dressing the Part edited by Claudia Brush Kidwell, also a Curator of the Division of Costume of the National Museum of American History, and Valerie Steele of the Fashion Institute of Technology ($24.95)

Corset, 1880's

Sequined evening dress, 1925

Nobody's Coming To Dinner Party

PAULA KASSELL

"The future of The Dinner Party is in great doubt right now," said Judy Chicago in a telephone interview from her Santa Fe studio a few days after she cancelled her gift of the art work to the University of the District of Columbia. Chicago withdrew the art work after it became embroiled with student protests against the way the university was run.

Protests were fueled by a misinformation campaign started by the Reverend Sun Myung Moon's "Washington Times", which asserted that The Dinner Party depicts female genitalia.

"We've discovered that the power of our opponents to spread misinformation is much greater than our power to reach people with the truth," Chicago said. Pat Mathis, a university trustee, sounded the same complaint. "It has been impossible to counter the lie, repeated over and over again. The students were made to believe that allocating $1.6 million of the District of Columbia budget to renovate the Carnegie Library where The Dinner Party was to be housed would somehow deprive the students of a better education," Mathis explained. "In addition, a right-wing member of the university faculty senate pressured other senate members to vote against Chicago's gift, saying they might lose their jobs if the university lost $1.6 million in operating expenses. In my view, history will show that the kids were totally manipulated by right-wing faculty members working with other on Capitol Hill. The Dinner Party was a victim of religious right-wing fanatics."

Chicago estimated that The Dinner Party would recoup in one year the university's expenditures in renovating the Carnegie Library. She told New Directions for Women that a $1.25 million gift from an admirer of The Dinner Party had already been received toward a matching grant. "At no time was it ever conceived that a single cent of federal dollars would be used," Mathis said.

On July 26, in a debate, members of the House of Representatives described The Dinner Party as "pornographic" and "obscene." Representative Stan Parris (R-VA) offered an amendment to the District of Columbia appropriation bill deleting $1.6 million from the University of the District of Columbia's 1991 budget. A widespread grass roots lobbying campaign that grew out of the national support of The Dinner Party convinced the Senate to restore the funds cut by the House.

The Dinner Party is a multimedia work of art in the form of an equilateral triangle 48 feet on each side. It tells the symbolic history of women in Western civilization through a series of 39 place settings for women who have made important contributions to women's rights, from the primordial mother goddess Gaia to the writer Virginia Woolf. The table sits on the Heritage Floor, composed of 2300 hand-cast, lustred porcelain tiles which bear the names of 999 women, whose lives and work form the foundation for the achievements of the women represented on the table. Chicago's plate designs depict open flowers or abstract oval patterns, which some interpret as suggesting the labia and the clitoris.

After a ten-year worldwide tour, The Dinner Party became too fragile to continue to travel. The board of Through the Flower (the nonprofit arts organization that cares for and maintains the work) began to discuss several proposals for permanent housing. The University of the District of Columbia was planning to develop the Carnegie Library in downtown Washington as a multi-cultural arts institution and a repository for art and archival material of peoples engaged in historic struggles for freedom. The board of Through the Flower and Judy Chicago saw this as a place where The Dinner Party could be seen by thousands of people, serve as a base for educational programs, and also be a part of a larger human effort for enfranchisement and dignity. That is why the artist gifted The Dinner Party to the university.

"As an artist," says Chicago, "I feel that my intentions, my integrity and my vision have been violated by the weight of the incessant misrepresentation campaign waged by those who would deny freedom of expression; they have managed to create a division of values where there is none—between the concept of The Dinner Party and the issues that are important to the students.

"As my life's work has been dedicated to the self-determination of all peoples, we withdrew the gift in support of the students right to determine their own destiny.

"It is vital that we understand the symbolic meaning of the assault on The Dinner Party", Judy Chicago emphasizes. "It was aimed at preventing our achievements from entering history. It is also important to realize that the suppression of The Dinner Party represents a significant escalation of the attack on art and artists. If this work, which has attracted a million viewers, and is taught in art history classes around the country, can be eclipsed, what does that mean about where we are in history?"

Still Not The Newspaper It Should Be

THE GIRLS IN THE BALCONY: Women, Men, and The New York Times by Nan Robertson (Random House) $22.

PAULA KASSELL

Nan Robertson was already a star reporter when she joined The New York Times' Washington bureau in 1963 and became one of "the girls in the balcony." Referring to the balcony of the National Press Club, Robertson uses it as a metaphor to symbolize women's place at the Times. Women reporters were not permitted to set foot inside the National Press Club until 1955, and even then they were only allowed into the balcony during the famous press club luncheons where world leaders and news makers spoke regularly. Not only did the women not get anything to eat, they did not even have chairs to sit on—the balcony was too narrow and crowded—nor could they ask questions of the speakers. Only in 1971 were women finally admitted as members.

Robertson details the history of women's accomplishments and frustrations at the Times, complete with telling anecdotes, in this remarkably short book without a wasted word. She covers the lives and careers of talented, idiosyncratic Times women past and present, and some of the men who helped or stymied them.

About half of Robertson's book is devoted to the women's discrimination suit against the Times, starting the day in 1969 when Grace Glueck read a list of promotions and wrote a note to the publisher asking, "Why were no women included?" He responded the next day: Point well taken and promised to consult with key management executives. She never heard another word. Robertson goes on to describe the founding luncheon of the Women's Caucus on Feb. 1, 1972, the filing of the suit in 1974, the decision of the Times management to settle the suit the very day it was to go to trial on Oct. 6, 1978—to forestall the airing of the very dirty Times' linen uncovered in the pre-trial discovery process.

The settlement gave monetary awards to 550 women, and the Times obligated itself to place significant numbers of women at every level in every news and business department, with specific interim goals and ultimate goals for all job categories. The court order specified that all this was to be accomplished in four years, from Jan. 1, 1979, to Dec. 31, 1982. The Times was directed to give the Women's Caucus yearly reports on its progress.

Some of the results were hard for the Times to justify as compliance. In four business categories, for example, the percentages of females actually declined during the settlement period, while other categories attained or surpassed their goals. The caucus considered taking the Times back into court but never did. The pain of the process was too debilitating, with the prime movers burned out and the younger women not willing to put their careers on the line and see them derailed like those of Betsy Wade and Joan Cook, two caucus leaders who pushed the suit.

Moving along swiftly from one eye-opening story to another, **The Girls in the Balcony** paints a kaleidoscopic picture of the most important newspaper in the world up to today. It is a different paper and a different place for women now. The stalled careers of the plaintiffs in the suit are in distinct contrast to the progress of the women who came after them. When the Women's Caucus celebrated the 10th anniversary of the settlement in 1988, the women who spoke included the national editor, the Sunday business editor, the picture editor, a member of the editorial board, a columnist (a former deputy metropolitan editor), the reporter covering the Supreme Court of the United States and several managers from the business side of the paper. Half of the speakers had been hired after the suit was filed.

I was a close observer of this progress. During the settlement years I was briefed by the Women's Caucus and then reported to the Times' shareholders at annual meetings, telling of the uneven compliance record, especially at the higher levels. On the dais were the all-white male officers who one by one were forced to admit to the hundreds of shareholders assembled that not one woman reported to them. By confronting the officers at the shareholders' meeting in 1986, I was able to bring to fruition another long-standing aim of mine and the caucus—to get the **Times** to use "Ms.," instead of pasting either "Miss" or "Mrs." before every woman's name, accurate or not, distasteful to her or not.

What is news? What makes page one? Who reports the events? Historically, women's opportunities to make the important decisions at the **Times** have been slight. Today, even in some meaningful top slots, they are only slightly greater. The **Times** is still not the best newspaper it could be. ▲

FAMILY PHOTOGRAPHS
(pages 31–35)

1. My parents, Bertha and Daniel Kassell (Atlantic City, NJ, 1920s)
2. As a Junior (Barnard College, 1938). Credit Delar Studios
3. With my husband, Gerson Friedman (honeymoon, Atlantic City, NJ, 1941)
4. My sister Beatrice with Harris Friedman, her fiancé—my husband Gerson's brother (Lake Hopatcong, NJ, 1940)
5. With Gerson's and my children, Daniel and Claire Friedman, in our front yard (Dover, NJ, 1946). Credit Gerson Friedman
6. With Gerson, reading to our grandchildren, Michael and Julia Foodman (Reading, MA, 1980). Credit Claire Friedman
7. My daughter, Claire Friedman, and her husband, Martin Foodman, in their kitchen (Reading, MA, 1990). Credit Judy Peretz
8. My son, Dan Kassell, with his wife, Cassandra Wallis Kassell, at their wedding reception (New York City, 1996)

FEMINIST CAREER PHOTOGRAPHS
(page 64)

1. Working as editor and publisher of the new feminist periodical *New Directions for Women in New Jersey* (Dover, NJ, 1972). Credit Dan Kassell
2. Publicity shot (1975)
3. Still working on *New Directions for Women,* now a national periodical (Dover, NJ, 1990). Credit John Bell
4. Featured in the Morris County Historical Society exhibit on New Jersey Feminists (Morristown, NJ, 2000–2001). Credit Dan Kassell

Appendix 1

POINT OF VIEW

Sending sons and daughters into combat

By PAULA KASSELL
Special to the Daily Record

When our sons are drafted and sent into combat to kill and to be killed and maimed themselves — and our daughters are not — is it our sons or daughters who are the victims of sex discrimination? Both, of course. My son and my daughter are equally precious to me, so it is impossible for me to understand how other mothers, along with fathers, politicians, lawmakers and generals, can accept sending only their boys off to battle. But they have, for thousands, perhaps millions, of years.

Sad and reluctant though the mothers and all the others may be, the calmness with which they assent to male military duties is in striking contrast to the emotional agitation roiled up by mental pictures of women on the battlefield. Yet we have seen the horrible sufferings of women and children in the wars and revolutions far from our shores. Villages and cities behind the lines are obviously not protected. Can we in the United States be confident, no matter how many billions of dollars we spend, that there is or ever will be a defense to ensure the safety of all our villages and cities?

So what are we protecting women from by excluding them from combat? Training for high-paying jobs, for one thing. In recent years the rules of the various services have seesawed between expanding and limiting the number of women they will admit and between opening and closing jobs to women. For instance, in 1983 the Army decided to bar women from 61 military specialties, adding 23 to the 38 already off limits. Among the additional jobs closed to women were carpentry, masonry, plumbing and electrical work — on the ground that these jobs might involve women soldiers in combat.

It reminds me of the "protective" labor laws repealed in the early 1970s. They barred women from working more than a specified number of hours per day or per week (which effectively "protected" women against overtime pay), or from working during late-night hours (but of course nurses, office cleaners and other low-paid women who worked all night at jobs not desired by men were exempted), or from lifting over a certain weight, sometimes as low as 15 pounds. (Hadn't the lawmakers ever seen a woman lift a toddler or a laundry basket?)

The military assigns its jobs in three broad categories: combat arms, combat support and combat service support. Analysis by the Women's Equity Action League shows that women are accepted in combat service support roles (such as medical, finance and personnel). No women are assigned to the combat arm of any service. There is no consistency among the services in the assignment of women in combat support roles (such as communications, intelligence and transportation).

The original goal of the combat exclusion laws was to protect women from combat. However, today's military doctrine calls for initial deep strikes into the rear of a battle zone to knock out the supply and service base of an enemy, leaving no safe place. While no longer protecting women, the combat exclusion laws impede their career advancement in the military. Many assignments currently classified as combat are necessary for promotion into top leadership positions.

A national debate on the role of women in the military could develop in 1987 when Congress considers new legislation sponsored by Senators William Proxmire (D-Wisconsin) and William Cohen (R-Maine). With public opinion against reinstatement of a draft and projections of a declining availability of young males over the next 10 years, the military will have to rely more and more on qualified females.

The Equal Rights Amendment is also again before Congress, and its effect on drafting women could once more prove to be a highly charged stumbling-block.

Strange that the ERA is rarely seen as a way of protecting men against the discrimination of combat. The horror of sending our young daughters into battle are so clear. It's a pity we as a nation don't love and protect our sons as fiercely.

Paula Kassell was the founder and first editor of the national feminist newspaper, New Directions for Women, and is now an associate editor and member of the publication's editorial board.

Sad and reluctant though the mothers and all the others may be, the calmness with which they assent to male military duties is in striking contrast to the emotional agitation roiled up by mental pictures of women on the battlefield.

Daily Record/DEB POLSTON

Courtesy of the Daily Record

Daily Record, February 15, 1989

Dear Susan: ERA still on schedule

Paula Kassell
OPINION SHAPERS

Today is Susan B. Anthony's birthday. Women got the right to vote in 1920, the centennial of her birth.

The campaign for women's suffrage took 72 years. The first Women's Rights Convention in 1848 came out with a Declaration of Sentiments modeled on the Declaration of Independence: "We hold these truths to be self-evident: that all men and women are created equal . . ." and included a demand for the ballot.

But during the Civil War women were urged to abandon their cause, and they did, campaigning vigorously instead for the 13th Amendment abolishing slavery. Nevertheless the word "male" appeared in the Constitution for the first time in the 14th Amendment guaranteeing rights for the new freed men. Next the women were frustrated when they campaigned to add "sex" to the 15th Amendment, prohibiting denial of suffrage on account of race.

So in 1869, Anthony and Elizabeth Cady Stanton, the other 19th century mother of women's rights, founded the National Women's Suffrage Association. They also started The Revolution, an independent women's newspaper with the motto, "Men, their rights and nothing more; women, their rights and nothing less." (What could be fairer?)

Anthony registered to vote and voted in the 1872 presidential election, through the cooperation of a sympathetic male registrar. For this illegal act she was indicted and brought to trial. Since women were considered incompetent to testify in court, she was not permitted to testify in her own defense and was found guilty.

The judge made the mistake of asking Anthony if she had anything to say before he pronounced sentence. After repeatedly trying to silence her, he fined her $100 and costs. She refused to pay even one dollar.

She spurned six offers of marriage so she could devote her life to gaining the vote for women. She told one suitor he would have to be willing to wait until her work for women's rights was finished. He declined.

Susan B. Anthony died at 86 in the upstairs bedroom of the 11-room Rochester, N.Y. house that was her home for 40 years. She spoke her last public words at her 86th birthday celebration shortly before her death in 1906: "Failure is impossible."

Immediately after getting the ballot in 1920, the National Women's Party (founded by Alice Paul of Moorestown and others in 1913) started urging an Equal Rights Amendment to the Constitution. The reason: U.S. courts consistently refused to include women under the definition of persons protected under the 14th Amendment.

The ERA was first introduced in Congress in 1923 and reintroduced for 49 years until it finally passed and was sent to the states in 1972.

Although the ERA was ratified by states representing the numerical majority of the population, and polls show that the majority of Americans favor it, the deadline for ratification expired in 1982 with the amendment still three states short of ratification. It has been reintroduced in every Congress since. Its history shows a striking parallel to the campaign for the ballot.

The timetable for the right to vote: proposed in 1848, first introduced in Congress in 1878, passed by Congress in 1919, ratified in 1920. Elapsed time: 72 years.

The timetable for the Equal Rights Amendment: proposed in 1920, first introduced in Congress in 1923, passed by Congress in 1972, not ratified yet. Elapsed time to date: 69 years.

Failure is impossible is a good motto.

Here is the complete text of the Equal Rights Amendment:

"Section 1. Equality of rights under the law shall not be denied or abridged by the United States or by any State on account of sex.

"Section 2. The Congress shall have the power to enforce, by appropriate legislation, the provisions of the Article.

"Section 3. This Amendment shall take effect two years after the date of ratification."

What could be fairer?

— *Paula Kassell of Dover, a retired analyst for Bell Laboratories, is a member of the Daily Record Opinion Shapers board. Opinion Shapers columns appear on Wednesdays.*

Reprinted courtesy of the Daily Record

Paula Kassell

25 West Fairview Avenue • Dover, New Jersey 07801 • 201-366-6036

February 24, 1989

Mr. William M. Donnellon, Editor
Daily Record
629 Parsippany Road
P. O. Box 217
Parsippany, NJ 07054

Dear Bill,

Purposely having let over a week go by since my Opinion Shapers piece ran on February 15, I am still incensed about the head. How could you allow the implication that because getting the ballot took 72 years, 69 years of not passing the ERA was "on schedule"?

The whole point to drawing the parallel between suffrage and the ERA was the outrageous number of years required, not the normality of it.

Having observed over the years many an excellent article about an issue of the feminist movement topped by a snide head, I included a suggested head in the attempt to prevent just what happened. All the preceding Opinion Shapers were dummied on five columns, so it was too long for the four-column format of mine. But my suggestion could easily have been cut to fit even using the same words. For instance, from my head, "S. B. Anthony said it all: Failure is impossible" to "Anthony said it all: Failure is impossible." Or: "Susan B. Anthony: "Failure is impossible. For sure, the use of her first name, "Dear Susan," is demeaning in the context of the historical piece I wrote.

Sincerely,

Paula

Note: The head that ran was: "Dear Susan: ERA still on schedule"

Daily Record
MORRISTOWN NEWSPAPERS, INC.

March 13, 1989

Paula Kassell
25 West Fairview Avenue
Dover, New Jersey 07801

Dear Paula,

It's taken me awhile to recover from your letter complaining about the headline on your column. Now that I've had a chance to compose myself, here goes.

I admit it. I wrote the headline. As a matter of fact, it was a rewrite of the one you suggested. And you may find it hard to believe, but there was neither a snide nor demeaning thought in my head when I wrote it.

My only idea was this: The popular thinking out there is that the ERA is dead. Your column pointed out that it's not dead, and that in the sweep of history, it's proceeding no more slowly than getting the ballot did. I wanted to get that idea across--not to say whether it's good or bad that it's taking so long, just that it's still moving along. That was it.

The headline didn't seek to say it's OK that it's taking so long. As a matter of fact, the phrase "on schedule" may have been more than a little sarcastic, taking a poke at how slow the process has been.

As for the use of "Susan" in the headline, I'm afraid I don't understand what you're saying. I used the first name, instead of the last, so the reader would know what I was talking about. If Susan B. Anthony did not have a last name that was the same as the first name of a man, I might have done it differently. (I tried to get the "B." in there but it wouldn't fit.)

Charles McDowell, the fine columnist of the Richmond Times-Dispatch, observes that all good writing should read as if it were a letter to a good friend. That's the feel I got from your column, and that's what I was seeking in the headline.

(Would the use of the name "Abe" in a hed on a piece about Lincoln or "George" above a piece about Washington be considered "demeaning"? I reserve the right to be enlightened.)

Daily Record
MORRISTOWN NEWSPAPERS, INC.

Let me close with the confession that I am perfectly capable of writing a lousy headline. I've done it before and I'll probably do it again. I may have done it this time. I do have a little trouble, however, with the implication that I am one of a legion of journalistic conspirators who have for years been trying to torpedo the feminist movement by topping "excellent" articles with "snide" headlines. That's a bit much.

I'll do better next time.

Cordially,

William M. Donnellon
Editor

Appendix 2

Biography from *Past and Present: Lives of New Jersey Women* (1990)
By Suzanne Messing

PAULA KASSELL, 1917–

Paula Sally Kassell, founder of the national feminist newspaper *New Directions for Women,* was born on December 5, 1917, in New York City, the younger of two daughters of Daniel and Bertha (Jaret) Kassell. Her parents were both native New Yorkers. Daniel Kassell, largely self-educated, was a stockbroker. He was also a self-taught musician who played the violin, the piano, and the mandolin and was an expert bridge player. Bertha (Jaret) Kassell was a homemaker who was active in community organizations. When Kassell was six, the family moved to Yonkers, NY, where she lived until she married in 1941.

Kassell attended public elementary school and Yonkers High School. As a child and teenager she often accompanied her mother to the Jewish Home for the Blind, a short distance from the family home. There she played with the blind children and later read to them and helped them with their homework. This experience awakened an interest in helping others that remained with her and resulted in a brief career in social work.

Daniel Kassell was ambitious for his daughters. At a time when relatively few women went to college, there was never any question that his two daughters would go. Both sisters went to Barnard College. Kassell graduated in 1939, with a major in psychology and sociology.

At college her feminist consciousness took root; according to Kassell, Barnard, under the leadership of Virginia Gildersleeve, was a heady place for a young woman. Students were imbued with ambition. It was also here that Kassell read and was greatly influenced by Margaret Mead's book *Sex and Temperament in Three Primitive Societies,* which introduced her to the thesis that society, not nature, determined sex roles and even temperament.

After college, Kassell worked briefly for the Yonkers, NY, Relief Department. On August 16, 1941, she married Gerson Friedman and moved to Dover (Morris County), NJ, where she has lived ever since. (Beatrice, her sister, married Gerson Friedman's brother.) A son, Daniel, was born in 1942, and in 1946 a daughter, Claire, was born. On her marriage Kassell said, "There can be no such thing as an equal marriage in our society, but mine was certainly among the most feminist." Her husband not only helped raise the children, he contributed many hours of work to *New Directions for Women*. He died April 21, 1986.

After the birth of the children, Kassell worked in the social welfare field for a while, but then chose to stay home and raise her family. By the time she was ready to seek employment again in 1955, she had lost some of her interest in social work. With encouragement from her husband, she became a technical editor at a company that did research on rocket motors, and then at Bell Telephone Laboratories, where she stayed until 1970. When she re-entered the job market she used her birth name at work and her husband's name socially. Gradually she used her own name more and more until she was using it exclusively.

In the early 1960s a new feminist voice began to make itself heard in American society. In 1966 the National Organization for Women (NOW) was formed. As soon as Kassell heard about it, early in 1967, she joined. NOW did not yet have local chapters. Kassell had already begun her feminist work as a member of the Women's Equity Action League. Her first project was to convince local newspapers to integrate help wanted ads. Previously, newspapers had published separate sections labeled "Help Wanted, Male" and "Help Wanted, Female."

In 1970 Kassell became dissatisfied with her job at Bell Laboratories because "Essentially we were working for the military. This was not bettering the world." At the same time, Marge Wyngaarden, a New Jersey feminist leader, was trying to bring together feminists from all parts of the state. When Kassell heard of this effort she suggested that a conference be held that would bring out potential recruits to the movement. It was decided to hold the conference at Fairleigh Dickinson University in Madison. Thus Kassell became coordinator of New Jersey's first statewide feminist conference, held on May 1, 1971. Called "New Directions for Women in New Jersey," it attracted 350 participants.

After the conference, the organizers decided to spend $240 in profits on a newsletter so that New Jersey women interested in feminism could stay in touch with each other. Kassell agreed to be editor. The first issue of *New Directions for Women in New Jersey,* a fourteen-page mimeographed bulletin, appeared on January 1, 1972. It was the first statewide feminist publication in the United States. The second issue, in November 1972, was an eighteen-page typeset tabloid. Enough advertising was sold to cover printing costs. In February 1973 it became a quarterly. That same year, Kassell and Marilyn Grant founded the Lakeland chapter of NOW, which later became the Morris County chapter.

In the spring of 1975 "New Jersey" was dropped from the title of the newspaper and *New Directions for Women* began to be distributed nationally. In 1980 it became a bimonthly with a circulation of 50,000. Set up as a non-profit enterprise, it is written, edited, and managed by paid and volunteer personnel.

Since its inception, *New Directions for Women* has sought to cover the whole spectrum of feminist activity, focusing especially on stories not likely to be covered adequately by the mainstream press. In its news pages, *New Directions for Women* has covered the political, legal, economic, and social issues that affect women. Articles on health and the arts appear regularly. Since 1972, an extensive book review section has been a feature in every issue.

Kassell was editor-publisher until 1977, when she resigned because of back problems brought on by the long hours and responsibilities of running the paper. Her title became associate editor and, in 1987, senior editor (Kassell, letter, July 20, 1987), and she remained on the Board of Trustees and the Editorial Board. She also continued to write a column on employment, "Equal Pay," as well as occasional editorials and book reviews.

Although Kassell was freed from daily responsibility for the paper, she remained involved with women's media. She became the United Nations representative for the Women's Institute for Freedom of the Press, a national association of media women and media-concerned women of which she is vice-president. She has also participated in the organization's efforts to set up a national and international women's news service, attending international conferences on women's media in Copenhagen, at the United Nations, and in Washington, D.C. She contributed a chapter on these efforts to *Communications at the Crossroads: The Gender Gap Connection* (1988).

In 1980 Kassell bought ten shares of stock in the New York Times Company; her investment was made with a purpose. She attended stockholder meetings, each time raising issues of interest to feminists, especially the advancement of women employees in all departments at the *Times*. At the April 30, 1986, meeting she brought up the use of the honorific "Ms." in the *Times'* pages. Long after most major newspapers had started to use Ms., the *Times* adamantly refused to do so, despite staff protests and letters to the editor from Kassell and others. At the meeting the publisher, Arthur Ochs Sulzberger, agreed to challenge the editorial staff to debate the issue. About a month later Kassell received a letter from Sulzberger stating "amidst great cheers from the women (and many of the men) who serve as reporters and editors of *The New York Times,* the attached notice was posted on the bulletin board: Beginning today (June 19, 1986), *The New York Times* will use Ms. as an honorific in its news columns." Eliminating sexist language from the media was a long-term issue on Kassell's agenda. Her effect on the *Times* was given widespread attention.

Farsighted and idealistic, Kassell is soft spoken and conservative in appearance. Called ladylike and traditional as well as feminist to the core by her friends, she describes herself as very determined and persistent. Quick to give credit to others, one of her most frequently used phrases is "I wasn't the only one."

Dr. Donna Allen, president of the Women's Institute for Freedom of the Press in Washington, D.C., and a long-time colleague of Kassell, said of her: "She never attacks. She takes what is strong and good about people and ideas and ignores the rest. She's a builder. Perhaps her greatest strength has been her sense of where things are going and where they should go. She recognizes the time to act. She has been in the forefront of women's media."

PAULA KASSELL ALWAYS TOOK WOMEN IN NEW DIRECTIONS
Women's e-News Journalist of the Month, December 1003

By Betsy Wade, WEnews Correspondent

(adapted and edited)

Paula Kassell, the Bronx-born suburban dweller founded and ran *New Directions for Women*, a national feminist newspaper with an ultimate circulation of 65,000.

But the achievement for which Kassell is best known—she is sometimes rueful that it overshadows other major efforts—was her ultimately successful struggle to get *The New York Times* to use the honorific "Ms." in place of the maritally discriminatory "Miss" and "Mrs," titles the paper clung to until 1986.

Kassell conducted the battle in a way typical of her—in a reasonable tone of voice, in a logical place—in front of *The Times'* annual stockholders meeting and through correspondence with Arthur Ochs Sulzberger Sr., then the publisher. On her own initiative she had bought 10 shares of Times stock solely to permit her to raise feminist issues in a well-reported forum; she had for years been consulting with the women's caucus at *The Times* about strategy on this and other matters.

In their lives, all feminist publications have had to scramble to increase paid circulation. Kassell took some imaginative routes. An early issue was distributed in bulk, free, to the New Jersey State Conference of the National Education Association. *New Directions for Women* also got a modest Ford Foundation grant to increase circulation, particularly among non-white readers. At one point, the paper had workers under the federal Comprehensive Employment and Training Act, who were on the job learning about publishing.

Kassell joined the National Organization for Women in 1967, the year after it was set up, and in 1973 created what became the Morris County Chapter in New Jersey. She is also the vice president and conference organizer for the Women's Institute for Freedom of the Press, a Washington non-profit.

Kassell, aware of the needs of researchers still unborn, created two cumulative indexes for her publication that provide a priceless tool to the issues raised over 22 years of the "second wave" of feminism. Her subject headings make archivists' hearts sing: "Child Care," "Violence," "Crime and Prison," "Comics," Spirituality," "Language," and dozens of others.

Following *The Times*'s capitulation on the use of Ms. in 1986, she wrote the story for the front page of *New Directions for Women*. She did not say that the day of the stockholders' meeting was only nine days after her husband of 45 years died. Asked about this circumstance in an interview, she said that her husband had always supported her work for feminist causes, and "the time was right" for another challenge on *The Times'* refusal to use "Ms.," so she set her grief aside and went ahead.

Among the many awards she has won, she is especially proud of:

> First recipient of the Millicent McIntosh Feminism Award Barnard College, The Women's College of Columbia University, New York City, 2004
>
> Medal of Honor, Veteran Feminists of America, 1998
>
> Woman of Achievement Award, Douglass College, The Women's College of Rutgers The State University, New Brunswick, New Jersey, 1994
>
> First Feminist Award, New Jersey Chapter, National Organization for Women, 1985

Betsy Wade worked for *The New York Times* for 45 years and was an active member of its women's caucus.

FEMINIST ACTIVITIES OF PAULA KASSELL

Paula Kassell describes herself as "a lifelong feminist of high ideals working toward a society that does not try to put anyone in a mold."

AT PRESS TIME

Vice President, Women's Institute for Freedom of the Press, Washington, D.C.

Member and Program Consultant, Morris County (NJ) National Organization for Women TV Task Force

Just published: *Taking Women in New Directions: Stories from the Second Wave of the Women's Movement from* New Directions for Women 1972–1993—*The Issues that Galvanized Women to Change Society Completely & Forever* (Hudson House)

BIOGRAPHIES

Every year in:
- Marquis *Who's Who of American Women*
- Marquis *World Who's Who of Women*
- Marquis *World Who's Who of the World*

Past and Promise: The Heritage of New Jersey Women—biographical essay (Scarecrow Press, 1989)

Featured in exhibit on New Jersey feminists by Morris County (NJ) Historical Society, September 2000 to March 2001

Journalist of the Month on women's e-news, www.womensenews.org, December 2002

PROFESSIONAL AND PERSONAL PAPERS

Deposited at their request in the National Women and Media Collection, University of Missouri School of Journalism, Columbia, Missouri

AWARDS (AS OF PRESS TIME)

First Feminist Action Award of New Jersey Chapter, National Organization for Women (November 1985). Presented to "the NOW-NJ activist whose political, professional and personal life best exemplifies the highest ideals of feminism."

Award for Feminist Achievement of Northern New Jersey Chapter, National Organization for Women (December 1986). Presented in "recognition of her key role in persuading *The New York Times* to use the honorific 'Ms.' and for her many outstanding contributions to the women's movement."

The Elizabeth Cady Stanton Award of the Women's Rights Information Center of Bergen County (NJ) (November 1993). Presented for "keeping up the momentum envisioned by Elizabeth Cady Stanton."

The Woman of Achievement Award of the New Jersey Federation of Women's Clubs and Douglass College of Rutgers University (March 1994). Citation: "Paula Kassell, a life-long activist, is a leader for women's rights on the state, national and international levels. Paula Kassell's contributions to women's causes are immeasurable, and citizens everywhere owe her a debt of gratitude for her splendid ongoing efforts on behalf of all women."

Award honoring achievements and contributions to feminist causes, from New Jersey Chapter, National Organization for Women (November 1995).

Veteran Feminists of America medal for continual activism in the feminist movement since the early 1970s (April 1998).

First recipient Millicent Carey McIntosh Feminism Award, from Barnard College of Columbia University (June 2004).

NOW New Jersey Foundation. Named as one of the "New Jersey Women Making History" (March 26, 2006)

BOOKS

"Planning an International Communications System for Women"—chapter in *Communications at the Crossroads: The Gender Gap Connection* (Ablex Publishing Corp., 1989)

"The Birth, Success, Death, and Lasting Influence of a Feminist Periodical: *New Directions for Women* (1972–1993)"—chapter in *Women Transforming Communications* (Sage Publications, 1995)

"*New Directions for Women*"—in *Women's Periodicals in the United States: Social and Political Issues* (Greenwood Press, 1996)

Taking Women in New Directions: Stories from the Second Wave of the Women's Movement from New Directions for Women *1972–1993—The Issues That Galvanized Women to Change Society Completely & Forever* (Hudson House, 2008)

INFLUENCE ON THE NEW YORK TIMES

As a *New York Times* stockholder, brought up issues of discrimination against women at *The Times* and spoke for the advancement of women at all levels, at several annual stockholder meetings, especially during the settlement period after the women's discrimination suit.

At the 1983 meeting I objected to *The Times* paying for dues and services at clubs that did not admit women members. The practice was stopped shortly thereafter.

At the 1986 meeting I brought up the refusal of *The Times* to use the honorific "Ms." About six weeks later, *The Times* began using "Ms."

ELEVEN CONFERENCES COORDINATED OR CO-COORDINATED

1979–84 - Five Annual Conferences on Planning a National and International Communications System for Women – sponsored by the Women's Institute for Freedom of the Press

1977 - New Jersey International Women's Year meeting – Program Chair and Vice Chair of the Committee (The Princeton Conference)

1976 - New Directions for Women in the Media: How to Market Your Executive Talents and Your Writings in Magazines, Newspapers and Books – sponsored by *New Directions for Women* and Rutgers School of Human Communications (at Douglass College)

1972 - Woman Power: A Force for Change – sponsored by New Jersey Chapter, National Organization for Women. At Newark State College (now Kean University)

1972 - Women and the New Professions of the '70s – for women high school students, math and science teachers and guidance counselors – sponsored by Stevens Institute of Technology

1972 - Affirmative Action for Women – sponsored by National Organization for Women. Attended by 150 New Jersey companies and unions

1971 - New Directions for Women in New Jersey – sponsored by New Jersey chapters, National Organization for Women and Fairleigh Dickinson University, Madison. *New Directions for Women in New Jersey* was founded as a follow-up to the conference

CAREERS

Founder, *New Directions for Women in New Jersey* (later *New Directions for Women,* a national periodical). A non-profit news periodical covering the feminist movement. Editor/Publisher 1971–77; Associate Editor 1977–87; Senior Editor 1987–93; Index Editor 1993–96. Publication ceased in 1993.

Technical Editor and Methods Analyst, Bell Telephone Laboratories (14 years)

Full-time mother and homemaker (14 years)

Caseworker and Foster Home Finder, Children's Aid Society, Newark (NJ)

Bidder's Representative Covering Picatinny Arsenal, Dover (NJ)

Investigator, Department of Home Relief, City of Yonkers (NY)

FORMERLY

Member, Media Committee, Forum '95 United Nations Conference on Women

Co-Convenor, Lakeland Chapter, National Organization for Women (later Morris County NOW)

Delegate, New Jersey State Board, National Organization for Women

Public Library Project Committee, New Jersey State Division on Women

Executive Vice President, Morris County (NJ) Grand Jurors Association

Psychiatric Social Worker, Greystone Park State Hospital (volunteer)

Vice President, Dover (NJ) Child Care Center

Girl Scout Troop Leader

Cub Scout Den Mother

MEMBERSHIPS

National, State and Morris County (NJ) National Organization for Women (NOW); National, State and Morris County (NJ) Women's Political Caucus; National Women's Hall of Fame; Alice Paul Institute; Coalition of Labor Union Women (Honorary Member); Older Women's League; National Women's Health Network; Comparable Worth Project; Gray Panthers; National Committee on Pay Equity; National Committee for Responsive Philanthropy; International Women's Media Foundation; Journalism and Women Symposium (JAWS); National Center for the Pro-Choice Majority; People for the American Way; Religious Coalition for Reproductive Choice; Voters for Choice; Judy Chicago's Through the Flower; National and State Abortion and Reproductive Rights Action League; Worthy Wage Campaign; American Journalism Historians Association; National Museum of Women in the Arts; Women in Military Service for America; Women for Racial and Economic Equality; Veteran Feminists of America; Center for Gender Equality; UNIFEM; Center for the Child Care Workforce; Planned Parenthood; Women's Campaign Fund; Institute for Women's Policy Research; National Breast Cancer Coalition; Center for Reproductive Law and Policy

EDUCATION

Studied for Master's Degree in Business Administration, Fairleigh Dickinson University, under Bell Laboratories Graduate Study Plan

Graduated from Barnard College, majors in psychology and sociology (1939)

Graduated from Yonkers (NY) High School (1935)

PERSONAL

Born New York City (Bronx) December 5, 1917

Married Gerson G. Friedman, a sales agent of the Equitable Life Assurance Society (1941). He died in 1986.

Widow; two children; two grandchildren

Appendix 3

The Birth, Success, Death and Lasting Influence of New Directions for Women (1972 - 1993 - ?)

By Paula Kassell
With invaluable contributions by Maurine Beasley, Phyllis Kriegel, Vivian Scheinmann, and Lynn Wenzel

The whole idea for starting *New Directions for Women in New Jersey* grew out of a conference of the same name held in the spring of 1971, sponsored by a coalition of women's rights groups in New Jersey. The proceeds of the conference ($240) were dedicated to starting a newspaper to "keep communicating" with the 300 women who had attended and to reach other potential feminists. Formerly a social worker and then a technical editor at Bell Telephone Laboratories, I was appointed editor and launched the publication with a volunteer staff in my Dover, New Jersey, home, working in two bedrooms furnished as offices and pasting up the newspaper on the dining-room table.

The first issue, the first statewide feminist periodical in the United States, came out in January 1972. Consisting of 14 mimeographed pages with a cartoon, it had a press run of 2,000 and was distributed, in addition to the feminist groups, to the presidents of as many different types of women's clubs in the state whose names we could get.

new directions for women in new jersey
Vol. 1 Number 1   January 1972

That first issue was very well received and highly praised. And we thought we would just have to sit back and the subscriptions would come rolling in—that anybody reading it would be inspired to write us a check for $3 for a year's subscription. But unfortunately only 85 people were so inspired. (As we learned later, 4.25 percent was actually a respectable return.)

And it never even occurred to us that we should have an aggressive circulation promotion policy. We talked about getting advertising for future issues without knowing how to go about it.

So, although we were supposed to be a quarterly, eight months went by before the idea came to me that was to get us enough money to put out another issue.

I began to see that if real changes were ever to take place, the women's movement would have to back up into the school system with a vigorous attack on the way schools were shunting girls into certain occupations and boys into others, starting in the very early grades. We decided to put out an education issue in the Fall of 1972 and distribute it free at the state teachers' convention to push the idea of equality in vocational education.

New directions for Women in New Jersey
Volume 1 Number 2   Fall 1972
through Volume 4 Number 1 Winter 1975

It was this burning desire to communicate our story to thousands of people that gave us our handle, both on increasing circulation and selling advertising. It suddenly came as a flash of inspiration that these two elements had to go together, that since we were distributing to teachers, librarians and library users, we had an ideal audience for book publishers. From this narrow base we were able to put together several hundred dollars worth of advertising from book publishers and a few feminist businesses.

We published an eight-page typeset tabloid with pictures, ordered a press run of 53,000, trucked it down to Atlantic City, and ended up with a deficit of only about $140.

The next issue, Winter 1973, was then created on the same principle. A special issue on employment and child care, we arranged to distribute it free to all members of the American Association of University Women and the Business and Professional Women in the state and the personnel managers of all the New Jersey companies employing 500 or more, a total of about 350 companies. This time we were able to sell several hundred dollars more in advertising than the previous issue, and this distribution increased our subscriber list several fold.

By 1975 we felt restricted in scope and potential subscribers by our statewide status, and decided to go national in coverage and circulation. We dropped "in New Jersey" from our logo. And with the Winter 1979-80 issue, we moved up to a bimonthly schedule after six years as a quarterly.

New directions for Women

Volume 4 Number 2 Spring 1975
through Volume 20 Number 4 July/August 1991

Our idealism was the secret of our success. *New Directions for Women* and all periodicals are always faced with two questions: Whom do we reach? What do they want to know? The marketplace gives one answer, of course—the only answer sought by periodicals whose purpose is to make money. But *New Directions for Women* was organized as a nonprofit corporation run by an unpaid board of trustees. It always had to be operated in a businesslike manner—subscriptions and advertising space had to be sold or the bills would not be paid and the venture would fail and disappear. But earnings and contributions were devoted solely to carrying out its ambitious objectives. Here is the "Statement of Purpose" published in the Fall 1972 issue:

New Directions for Women is a consciousness-raising organ published to inform women about equal rights.
New Directions for Women is directed to all women, not just feminists.
It is filled with hard news and reports on the issues that concern women rarely found in the standard press.
It is written to energize women to take action to advance their position.
New Directions for Women believes that when women understand sex discrimination, they will reach for the tools to combat it.

The key to the whole operation is to be found in the second paragraph of the "Statement of Purpose": "*New Directions for Women* is directed to all women, not just to feminists." We always tried to reach women who did not yet quite understand the feminist movement, a lack of understanding that often leads to fear.

Since its beginning in the mid-60s, the feminist movement has suffered from inadequate and inaccurate reporting and false interpretation by the standard media. The first and most notorious instance was the report that bras were burned in a demonstration at a Miss America contest in 1968. This episode NEVER TOOK PLACE, yet feminists are still trying to live down the epithet "bra burner." The important reason for the action that DID take place—girdles, bras and lipsticks were tossed in a barrel as symbols of the unnatural distortions of body, face, and mind that constrict women.

Page after page could be filled with further examples of inept or distorting coverage (or noncoverage) of women's events and issues in books, newspapers, magazines, radio and TV—and perhaps especially in advertising.

New Directions for Women was founded because constant, accurate, in-depth coverage of the issues as they surface and develop is possible only in a woman-run publication; our activism and contacts with feminists and feminist groups throughout the country enabled us to scoop the mainstream press time after time.

An excerpt from a successful subscription promotion letter of the mid-1970s tells the heart-warming story of our inspiration and devotion:

RECIPE [By Brenda Turner]
1 cup crushed ego
1 teaspoon job discrimination
1/4 teaspoon chauvinism
1 well-beaten path to the washing machine
1/2 teaspoon grated nerves
1 pinch from a man in the street
1 dash from the dentist to the babysitter

Mix all ingredients, one on top of the other, and stir violently. Cook until you feel a slow burn and add one last straw.

Serves: 53 percent of the population   Women are becoming aware of the ingredients that make up their daily lives, and many questions are rising to the surface.

The staff of *New Directions for Women* is dedicated to finding some answers and creating a newspaper that will affect every woman who reads it.... That is why we are trying to reach the woman who recognizes herself as a person, with her own rights even though she may have heavy responsibilities for others.

New Directions for Women, a nonprofit organization, is funded by subscriptions, advertising, a federal grant, and donations from feminist groups and individuals who want news about the women's movement to reach more women.

Of course, we rely heavily on advertisements, but we do have a firm policy to never accept one that we do not believe would be of positive value to our readers.

Most of our staff are volunteers: teachers, homemakers, lawyers, politicians, and secretaries, who joined us after reading *New Directions for Women*. Many are professional writers or artists who donate their work to us because they know they are helping other women.

The unusual dedication of the staff is one of the reasons why our subscribers feel a personal relationship with the women whose words they are reading.

We are reaching intelligent, concerned, involved women. A survey of our readers indicates that 79 percent are college educated, and 60 percent of these have continued their schooling in postgraduate work. 66 percent of our readers are employed full- or part-time. 49 percent are married.

In the survey our readers most often voted for our articles about Legal Rights, Job Opportunities, Legislation, and New Life Styles.

We are not afraid to publish articles on controversial subjects...

"Volunteerism—The Still Sizzling Bomb." The debates and demerits of volunteering, and the difference be-tween unpaid work that is "service-oriented" and "change-directed."

"Conference MDs Equate menopause With Sickness."
A report on the meeting that prompted our series on the menopause.

"How to Say No to a Rapist." There are two schools of thought: some believe a woman should resist violently; others say a woman must try to appease a rapist.

In the very first issue (January 1972) we reviewed 1971 rulings about abortion in New Jersey; told of President Richard Nixon's veto of a comprehensive child care bill that had passed both houses of Congress after much lobbying by women's groups (To this day 23 years later Congress has not passed another). The Spring and Summer 1993 issues carried helpful articles about divorce and alimony written by an attorney. Coverage of domestic violence started in 1976. Almost every issue from the beginning delineated the pervasive discrimination against women in employment but stressed earning money and getting ahead as the basis of women's liberation. Not forgetting the housewife, the Winter 1973 issue assessed her economic value in view of the 12 jobs she filled, which came to $1,000 per month in 1972 dollars for the more than 28 million working at the job.

Throughout its life the paper acted as a consciousness-raising conduit to the women's movement, covering the issues, always giving names and addresses of organizations to help women get involved and become activists. At the same time every issue had helpful information about personal problems—alcoholism starting in the Spring 1973 issue, sexual harassment as early as the Spring 1979 issue, questioning estrogen use in Summer 1974. Older women were given regular coverage starting with the Winter 1974 issue, and in 1978 *Prime Time*, a newsletter for older women, was absorbed by *New Directions for Women*, and coverage of aging and agism was increased.

The women who managed and wrote for the paper through the years were as varied as the people who read it, most strikingly in the age range—from the teens through the 70s. Many of the writers and staff gained professional stature and self-confidence. Learning to put out the paper was a growth experience no matter what the age or background. It would be safe to say that no women who gave herself to the venture was untouched by the experience.

The same could be said for hundreds, perhaps thousands, of *New Directions for Women* readers, judging by the flood of letters they sent throughout the years: "My feelings about myself have changed since I've read this paper." "Your paper has been most helpful to me in determining my future goals in life." "After reading your publication, I am sure I will find a way I might be able to assist in the efforts of other women." (This letter illustrates the conduit to activism at work.)

Now that I've painted that rosy picture, I must admit there are two very serious flaws in it.

We survived only because, through most of our years, the staff was almost entirely unpaid, and all the writers gave us their work free, even some professionals. They worked for *New Directions for Women* for nothing because of their strong convictions of its importance to the women's movement. But their regular jobs took precedence regardless of our deadlines. We had to increase our budget several fold to pay for staff work, pay our reporters, and pay for creative work (verse, cartoons, drawings and photographs).

The financial problem was tied in closely with our other major serious difficulty. Among the hundreds of women who have written or worked for *New Directions for Women* hardly anyone aside from myself took responsibility for the business side of the publication, the areas usually under the jurisdiction of the publisher rather than the editor.

Recognizing the imperative for women to face and learn to operate in the business world, in 1976 *New Directions for Women* organized a conference, "New Directions for Women in the Media: How to market Your Executive Talents and Your Writings in Books, Newspapers and Magazines." This conference also featured presentation to five women of the "*New Directions for Women* Positive Image of Women Award" and presentations of awards to the winners of our first essay contest, "A High School Student Looks at Equal Rights for Women." The second essay contest, in 1982, on the subject "What Do You Have to Say About Feminism," was a double contest—for women never before published, and for high school students. The third essay contest, in 1989, called a "feminist essay competition," specified "You may write about anything you wish, but it must be from a personal perspective."

We tried to use the media conference to recruit women to help on our business side, but this did not work out.

In spite of our business-side staffing problem, in its first few years the publication expanded in size, reaching 20 pages by November 1975. The size of each issue depended on the advertising space sold; the printing bill for each issue was covered by its ad revenue. Since paid subscribers now numbered in the thousands, and tens of thousands of copies of each issue were distributed free for circulation promotion, the ad rate was raised to $400 per page.

Our ad rate structure was unusual, devised in 1972 by my son, who was in advertising. On the assumption that most of the ad spaces we sold would probably be eight column inches or less, we needed to promote maximum revenue from small ads. So, rather than the usual flat rate per column inch, it was based on a sliding scale (the larger the ad, the lower the rate per inch). Advice from a woman buying advertising space for a major book publisher suggested a saleable price for a typical book ad in a periodical such as ours, and the rates above and below were extrapolated from that marker. Prices ranged from the minimum size offered (2 column inches) for $30 to a full page (a total of 80 column inches) for $320. My knowledgeable son's theory proved to be correct, and the sliding scale was retained as the full-page rate was raised:

to $400 per page in 1975 (circulation promised: 30,000, except education and book issue: 50,000)
to $500 per page in 1976 (same circulation figures)
to $550 in 1987 (circulation promised: 55,000)
to $600 in 1991 (circulation promised: 65,000)
to $675 in 1992 (same circulation figure).

Subscription rate changes were much more modest to keep the paper as affordable as possible. When we published our first issue in 1972, *New Directions for Women* (then a quarterly) was $3 per year. In 1987 we increased the price to $4 per year, or $1 per issue. When we went bimonthly in 1980, our annual rate went to $6, the price per issue remaining $1. Because of skyrocketing increases in the costs of doing business (printing, postage, mailing services), we raised the subscription rate to $10 per year in 1982.

Starting to pay the staff in the mid-1980s increased the budget by $1,000 an issue, and the subscription price was raised to $12 per year in 1989. In the late 1980s we started to pay writers (who got two cents a word), artists, and photographers, and in 1993 the subscription rate was raised to $16.

During the seven years that New Directions for Women was published in my home, I employed one paid clerk-typist, half-time. Late in 1975 we obtained a federal Comprehensive Education and Training Act (CETA) grant administered by the county for one full-time employee, salary and payroll taxes paid. We contracted to train a woman in the business side of publication and put the new staff member to work soliciting advertising and writing subscription and renewal letters. Since so much of the work involved book advertising, at the end of the grant period she found a responsible supervisory position in the advertising/publicity department of a book publisher.

By 1977 I was suffering from a painful muscle spasm in my back, diagnosed as due to tension, and could no longer take responsibility for editing and publishing the paper. The offices were moved to rented quarters in Westwood, New Jersey, initially setting up with borrowed card tables and chairs. Several volunteers who lived nearby agreed to run the paper cooperatively. Decisions were made by an editorial board and a board of trustees. I remained a member of both boards and continued to write for the paper. By 1978, after some of the women started full- or part-time paid employment, Vivian Scheinmann was appointed managing editor, with overall responsibility for both the business and editorial aspects. Scheinmann had a Masters in Library Service from Columbia University and administrative business experience. She had been children's book editor and then book editor of *New Directions for Women.*

"In retrospect," Scheinmann says, "we were very courageous, considering we were working with an unsalaried staff and with minimal advertising. However, the consensus was that we had to grow or we would stagnate; we knew we would also have to expand our coverage and proceed to a bimonthly publishing schedule." (January/February 1980 was the first bimonthly issue.)

At the time of the move the paper had about 8,000 paid subscribers—one third on the east coast, one third on the west coast, and the rest scattered across the country in every state. It was also sold at feminist bookstores.

Additional CETA grants were obtained, continuing until 1980, to train five minority women and displaced homemakers in the publishing business. One was responsible for subscription records, one learned to sell advertising space and greatly improved the revenue, one was office manager, a fourth did clerical work, and the fifth learned to be the bookkeeper. The subscription base and readership grew as the CETA staff applied themselves to succeeding in their individual goals and in those we had set for the paper. When the CETA grants ended, three of the employees found jobs in the private sector doing work for which we had trained them, and two became paid employees of *New Directions for Women.*

Vivian Scheinmann expended much time and effort to find new grant money. The stumbling block was that most foundations did not fund periodicals as a matter of policy. However, when she put together the training of women along with the expansion of *New Directions for Women* as a tool for education, the Ford Foundation approved a three-year grant totaling about $60,000. It was for a subscription campaign among minority women and to strengthen our financial position. Utilizing the grant, the publication was sent free to women in prisons and mental institutions as well as to university women's centers and women's clinics.

During Scheinmann's regime, a successful contribution campaign was carried on through ads in the paper requesting tax-deductible donations. Several premiums were pictured: a see-through bubble umbrella with the *New Directions for Women* logo for a $25 contribution, a canvas tote bag with the logo for $35, a pen on a marble stand engraved with either the logo or the donor's name for $50, a zippered leather case with 10 carpentry tools and the logo for $100, and a collapsible director's chair with steel frame and canvas seat and back for $500.

For the January/February 1982 issue, the trustees revised the "Statement of Purpose" to reflect the coming of age of the Second Wave of the feminist movement:

New Directions for Women is committed to publishing the many voices of feminism. We believe the diversity of the women's movement must be seen as one of its strengths.
New Directions for Women is a national feminist periodical written for feminists and committed to reaching out to those not yet dedicated to a feminist future.
New Directions for Women believes when we understand the pervasive force of sexism, we will act to effect change.

In addition to a strong book review section for adult and children's and young adult books and broad coverage of women in the arts, the paper covered, among other feminist issues, child abuse, domestic violence, prostitution, rape, homophobia, sexuality, politics, and local and national feminist actions and events. Columns took up health, legal, employment, and tax issues affecting women.

Although it always provided a feminist perspective, the paper was never allied with any particular group within the women's movement and sought to offer a broad spectrum of opinion, particularly on controversial issues such as pornography.

In 1983, Vivian Scheinmann left the paper to open a feminist book store with Pamela Sheldrick, who had been doing the *New Directions for Women* layout for several years. The paper moved its offices to an old building in Englewood, New Jersey, renovated for the Women's Rights Information Center of Bergen County. Phyllis Kriegel, a graduate of the women's history program at Sarah Lawrence College, became managing editor. According to Kriegel, when she took over, the publication had an annual budget of $43,000 compared to an annual budget of $157,000 in its final year. The increase reflected Kriegel's decisions to compensate staff members and contributors.

"We started to pay the staff in the mid-1980s, and in the late 1980s we started to pay writers (who got two cents a word), artists and photographers," she said in an interview in 1995. Although no one was ever employed more than part-time, "we were paying out an added cost of $1,000 per issue," she said. "We felt we could no longer ask women to be volunteers on a continuing basis. The times had changed. A lot of good writers we wanted wanted a token that they were professionals, and we honored that," she explained.

Even though articles were written by professionals, "We were careful to make the copy tight and lively," Kriegel commented. Unlike some other feminist newspapers that run submissions word for word, "We felt we had a literary and grammatical standard. We cared passionately about writing and how it sounded."

Kriegel said she contributed her own funds to hire a staff and to "help leverage other funds." Some years, she said, she gave a significant amount—$25,000 to $30,000. It was my life and I was delighted that I could do it."

By 1993, *New Directions for Women* had a readership of some 65,000 (a combination of paid and free distribution) and was a nationally and internationally recognized and respected agent of social change. Its size had grown to between 44 and 48 pages, with up-to-date style and professional design and layout by computer. This was accomplished, in part, by grants from the Ms. Foundation for Education and Communication, the Funding Exchange, ADCO Foundation, the Sophia Fund, North Star, the Foundation for a Compassionate Society, and the Harbach Foundation. But grants were sporadic and small. "A $2,000 to $3,000 grant for us was handsome," Kriegel said.

One gift was more substantial. *New Directions for Women* was distributed internationally starting in 1989-90 through a $30,000 grant for two years from Geneviève Vaughan, a philanthropist. The grant financed an international pull-out section called "Country of Women" that ran for three years and included material from a women's newspaper in Italy on feminist conferences in Europe. The section featured a quotation from Virginia Woolf: "As a woman I have no country. As a woman I want no country. As a woman my country is the whole world." *New Directions for Women* had a correspondent in Eastern Europe at the time of the collapse of communism, reporting on its effects on women.

A "Twentieth Anniversary Benefit Concert" was produced in 1991 at Steinway Hall in New York City. The Mannes Trio (the all-woman trio in residence at the Mannes College of Music) donated its services for an evening of classical "Music by Great Woman Composers." After expenses, which were largely donated, the concert added $2,250 to the paper's coffers.

Under Kriegel's leadership *New Directions for Women* ran a valuable intern/co-op program, drawing students of diverse backgrounds from many colleges and universities who were then trained and supervised by staff. The program was valuable to the paper, to the students, and to the community. Many of the interns went on to work for social change in the Peace Corps, politics, religious organizations, city government, hospitals, and clinics, as well as in journalism with mainstream magazines, newspapers, and publishing houses.

Beset by rising production costs and falling subscriptions, which had declined to about 3,500, *New Directions for Women* was forced to fold with the September/October 1993 issue. (Subscription fulfillment was taken over by another fine feminist periodical, *ON THE ISSUES.*) The subscription price, held at $10 for most of Kriegel's tenure, was $18 a year at the time publication ceased. Kriegel, who had prepared a business plan at the request of a woman's foundation, decided to end the operation, which advertised a total circulation of 65,000 (because of free distribution) after she failed to get expected funding.

Under Kriegel's leadership the paper stressed more investigative journalism. "We were far ahead of other publications," Kriegel feels. "We had a wonderful issue on women in prisons in the early 1990s. We were the ones telling the story of the grassroots woman's movement at a time when people said it was dead. We tackled what feminist think tanks say about feminists. We wrote about women's funding sources, social change, women's health, women losing their children. That was part of the problem—people said reading it was a downer. We were bringing a lot of bad news."

The paper also regularly covered lesbians, peace activism, and spirituality. A New York Metro Area Supplement was added in 1989, and news from the Women's Action Coalition was carried regularly starting early in 1993.

Kriegel believes lack of promotion led to the demise. "We never had enough money or talent to get on radio programs and be visible. I couldn't do it and run the paper," she said. "Book advertising was the largest source of advertising [and] we went up to $5,000 an issue in ads." Tying into editorial themes, the publication solicited advertising for issues on special topics like women's history, black history, and women's spirituality." Yet *New Directions for Women* lacked local circulation and, consequently, failed to attract local advertising.

Another problem was its newspaper format. Even though its bimonthly publication schedule made it hard to cover news events, "We attempted to be timely," Kriegel said. "We were a news magazine." Kriegel believes a gap has been left in the media since *New Directions for Women* went under.

But *New Directions for Women* will have a lasting influence on its staff, its writers, and on the changed lives and minds of its readers.

Almost unbearably touching were the many letters received after our final issue. A few excerpts: "Oh woe, alas—such sad news. I can only imagine what the loss is to you, for us it is a cruel cut indeed." "I wept when I read your letter yesterday. You have been friends of long-standing to me (collective 'you') for all the years as I read and watched *New Directions* evolve and become the excellent publication that it was." "It just breaks my heart to see such a wonderful periodical run out of funds and have to stop publishing." "No words I can think of will say what I felt when I read your letter about *New Directions for Women* lying down to rest. It's been a good friend for so long I never considered living without it." "For me your closing the windows is a cause for mourning. You have opened the many windows to the world's women for me. You have been my companion." "From my selfish perspective I'm grateful that you were around during the years I was most isolated in Topeka and *New Directions for Women* was my lifeline."

New Directions for Women has published two cumulative indexes of its complete contents: the Ten Year Cumulative Index of Volume 1 Number 1 through Volume 10 Number 6 (January 1972 through November/December 1981), and the Twelve Year Cumulative Index of Volume 11 Number 1 through Volume 22 Number 5 (January/February 1982 through September/October 1993, the final issue.)

The first index was compiled entirely by volunteers, with printing and binding donated by a major New Jersey corporation. Compiling the second index was partly paid work but mostly volunteer. Printing, binding and marketing funds were raised with a letter to *New Directions for Women's* loyal supporters.

Arranged chronologically by subject, the indexes provide a running account of feminist actions, philosophies, and feelings, issue by issue, year by year. Hundreds of articles are listed in the indexes under more than one subject to facilitate research on every aspect of the movement. In the first index there are 131 subject headings, 52 subject cross-references, listing of over 600 reviewed books (adult, children's, and young adult), over 300 advertisers in *New Directions for Women*, profiles of almost 50 feminist organizations, over 100 biographical profiles.

The second index adds many subjects that surfaced since 1981, such as: Addictions, AIDS, Backlash, Courts, Disabilities, Homelessness, Hunger, Incest, Peace Activism, Spirituality. There are 34 additional subject headings, 1900 book reviews, over 100 articles on women's health, 150 on international affairs, over 750 articles and reviews of Women in the Arts, including the performing arts, 120 biographical profiles, over 650 advertisers in *New Directions for Women*. The work of over 1000 writers and almost 500 graphic artists appeared in *New Directions for Women* during these twelve years.

Both indexes include the columns and regular features, such as: Media Watch, Women in the Arts, Equal Pay, Your Legal Problems, International Round-up and Country of Women, the Metro Section, Keeping Tabs on Our Health, Editorials, Calendars.

We believe this is the **only** cumulative index by subject of the many issues of the women's movement as they were documented by a feminist periodical. Evidence that the indexes are used rests on the several hundreds of dollars in royalties *New Directions for Women* is still receiving from University Microfilm International.

The archives of *New Directions for Women*—virtually the complete contents of all our files—are being deposited in the National Women and Media Collection at the University of Missouri School of Journalism in Columbia, Missouri, where these records will afford valuable insight into the workings of feminist journalism.

SO THE LEGACY OF *New Directions for Women* WILL LIVE ON.

When we started our feminist newspaper in 1971, we didn't realize we would be running a business, unbelievable as that seems to us today. In the 22 years we managed to keep publishing, we did a remarkable job of learning all the aspects of the business, but we never had the time, energy, funds—or inclination—to do all the necessary publicity and circulation promotion. Putting out the next issue always came first. And that is what finally brought us to our downfall in 1993.

We offer, to those who come after us, this detailed history of why we started and how we learned to become the most successful feminist newspaper in the country (called by *Magazines for Libraries* "the leading feminist newspaper in the United States"). Just as important to understand are the factors that thwarted us throughout our long history and that ultimately led to our demise as a publishing venture.

We hope that this chronicle of *New Directions for Women* will encourage, not dispirit, women who may be contemplating a new feminist periodical or are now publishing one. We hope that others will be inspired by the idealism that inspired us, by the conviction that accurate, in-depth coverage of women's lives and feminist issues as they surface and develop is possible only in a woman-run newspaper.

Appendix 4

ACKNOWLEDGMENTS

It is with pleasure that I acknowledge the dedication and contribution of the people who helped me with this book.

Dan Kassell, my son, for the preliminary cover design, technical advice on many aspects of the book, his encouragement and constant nagging to get the thing done.

Brenda Deming, my feminist friend, for her hours of work on the computer and innumerable tasks to complete the book and help with my daily life and chores.

Betsy Wade, for my biography on Women's e-news, January 2002, and reprinted in the book.

Suzanne Messing, for my biography in "Past And Present: Lives of New Jersey Women" 1990, and reprinted in the book.

Barbara Richer, for preliminary work on the cover design.

Laurie Pettine for the cover design.

Special thanks for permission to reprint cartoons, pictures, and drawings in *New Directions for Women*: Ruth Ahntholz, Brooklyn Museum of Arts, bulbul, Executive Female Digest published by the National Association for Female Executives.

The outstanding feminists whose enthusiastic comments on my work appear on the back cover and the inside back cover: Jacqui Ceballos, President, Veteran Feminists of America; Blanche Wiesen Cook, author, *Eleanor Roosevelt* (biography in three volumes); Sheila Gibbons, Editor, *Media Report to Women;* Janet Jakobsen, Director, Barnard Center for Research on Women; Susan Kaufman, Professor of Journalism, Eastern Illinois University; Cheris Kramarae, Director, Center for the Study of Women in Society, University of Oregon; Angela Rapkin, Professor, Women's Studies, University of South Florida (retired); Bernice Sandler, National Association for Women in Education; Kate Swift, co-author, with Casey Miller, of *Words and Women* and *The Handbook of Nonsexist Writing*.

Special thanks to Diana Drew and Robert Grayson of Stella Hart Public Relations for all their help in publicizing and promoting *Taking Women in New Directions*. Thanks, as well, to Hudson House for shepherding this manuscript to publication.

Taking Women in New Directions

- Fascinated by this chronicle of women's history?
- Captivated by how *New Directions for Women* reflected and ushered in the women's movement of today?
- Amazed at how feminism, as seen through the prism of these "You are there" pieces, dovetails with our country's evolving recognition of rights for everyone?

Purchase a copy for your daughter, your mother, your grandmother, your aunt, your husband, your son, your best friend, your activist neighbor, your co-workers . . .

Makes a terrific gift—thought-provoking, insightful, a joy to dip into again and again.

Just $15.95 apiece, plus $4 shipping & handling. Order four or more at a time and the price per book drops to $10.95 apiece, plus $4 shipping & handling to each address.

It's easy to order: Pay by credit card (the preferred method; call Hudson House, 845–463–1100 to place an order or send the publisher the completed form below), or send a check or money order to Hudson House, 675 Dutchess Tpke., Poughkeepsie, NY 12603.

Payment method: [ ] Visa   [ ] MasterCard   [ ] check enclosed [ ] money order enclosed

Credit card no.: _____ Exp. date _____

Ordered by:

Name_____   Name_____

Address _____   Address _____

_____   _____

Tel (   )_____ E-mail_____   Tel (   )_____ E-mail_____

Send ___ book(s) to the above address.   Send ___ book(s) to the above address.

Send ___ book(s) to the address below.   Send ___ book(s) to the address below.

Ship to:

Name_____   Name_____

Address _____   Address _____

_____   _____

Tel (   )_____ E-mail_____   Tel (   )_____ E-mail_____

No. of books ordered _____   Total $_____   No. of books ordered _____   Total $_____

Copy this order form to ship to additional addresses.

Taking Women in New Directions

- Fascinated by this chronicle of women's history?
- Captivated by how *New Directions for Women* reflected and ushered in the women's movement of today?
- Amazed at how feminism, as seen through the prism of these "You are there" pieces, dovetails with our country's evolving recognition of rights for everyone?

Purchase a copy for your daughter, your mother, your grandmother, your aunt, your husband, your son, your best friend, your activist neighbor, your co-workers . . .

Makes a terrific gift—thought-provoking, insightful, a joy to dip into again and again.

Just $15.95 apiece, plus $4 shipping & handling. Order four or more at a time and the price per book drops to $10.95 apiece, plus $4 shipping & handling to each address.

It's easy to order: Pay by credit card (the preferred method; call Hudson House, 845–463–1100 to place an order or send the publisher the completed form below), or send a check or money order to Hudson House, 675 Dutchess Tpke., Poughkeepsie, NY 12603.

Payment method: [ ] Visa   [ ] MasterCard   [ ] check enclosed [ ] money order enclosed

Credit card no.: _____   Exp. date _____

Ordered by:

Name_____ | Name_____

Address _____ | Address _____

_____ | _____

Tel (   )_____ E-mail_____ | Tel (   )_____ E-mail_____

Send ___ book(s) to the above address. | Send ___ book(s) to the above address.

Send ___ book(s) to the address below. | Send ___ book(s) to the address below.

Ship to:

Name_____ | Name_____

Address _____ | Address _____

_____ | _____

Tel (   )_____ E-mail_____ | Tel (   )_____ E-mail_____

No. of books ordered _____   Total $_____ | No. of books ordered _____   Total $_____

Copy this order form to ship to additional addresses.